The Virgo Book
Everything You Should Know About Virgos

CRAFTED BY SKRIUWER

Copyright © 2025 by Skriuwer.

All rights reserved. No part of this book may be used or reproduced in any form whatsoever without written permission except in the case of brief quotations in critical articles or reviews.

At **Skriuwer**, we're more than just a team—we're a global community of people who love books. In Frisian, "Skriuwer" means "writer," and that's at the heart of what we do: creating and sharing books with readers worldwide. Wherever you are in the world, **Skriuwer** is here to inspire learning.

Frisian is one of the oldest languages in Europe, closely related to English and Dutch, and is spoken by about **500,000 people** in the province of **Friesland** (Fryslân), located in the northern Netherlands. It's the second official language of the Netherlands, but like many minority languages, Frisian faces the challenge of survival in a modern, globalized world.

We're using the money we earn to promote the Frisian language.

For more information, contact : **kontakt@skriuwer.com** (www.skriuwer.com)

TABLE OF CONTENTS

CHAPTER 1: UNDERSTANDING VIRGO'S HISTORY AND SYMBOLISM

- Origins of the Virgo constellation
- Cultural myths and harvest themes tied to the maiden figure
- Planetary and elemental connections that shape Virgo's core

CHAPTER 2: TYPICAL VIRGO PERSONALITY TRAITS

- Key behavior patterns and strengths often seen in Virgo
- Role of Mercury and the Earth element in daily habits
- Balancing detail-focused thinking with emotional needs

CHAPTER 3: VIRGO IN ANCIENT STORIES AND LEGENDS

- Early star lore and mythic depictions of the maiden
- Links to goddesses of justice and agriculture
- Lasting impact of these tales on modern views

CHAPTER 4: VIRGO'S ELEMENT AND ITS INFLUENCE

- How Earth energy shapes Virgo's practical nature
- Mercury's swift reasoning paired with grounded outlook
- Connecting daily life to deeper Earth sign themes

CHAPTER 5: STRENGTHS THAT SHAPE THE VIRGO CHARACTER

- Detail-oriented approach that boosts accuracy
- Dependability and helpful attitudes in work or friendships
- Natural humility and steady skill-building

CHAPTER 6: COMMON CHALLENGES FOR VIRGO

- Perfectionism and the anxiety it can cause
- Overthinking and self-criticism in personal goals
- Ways to handle conflict or stress related to these traits

CHAPTER 7: VIRGO IN PERSONAL RELATIONSHIPS

- How Virgos connect with partners through acts of support
- Patience, trust, and caution in emotional sharing
- Balancing organized tendencies with others' comfort

CHAPTER 8: EMOTIONAL LIFE OF A VIRGO

- Managing sensitive feelings behind a calm front
- Finding healthy outlets for worry or tension
- Building deeper bonds through steady empathy

CHAPTER 9: VIRGO IN WORK AND CAREER

- Preferred roles that benefit from detail and logic
- Leadership style marked by planning and fairness
- Challenges with delegation and workplace stress

CHAPTER 10: VIRGO AT HOME AND DAILY LIFE

- Creating order in household routines
- Practical methods for chores and budgeting
- Blending comfort and neatness in personal spaces

CHAPTER 11: VIRGO'S APPROACH TO PHYSICAL WELL-BEING

- Organized diet and exercise habits
- Avoiding extremes in health routines
- Finding balance between discipline and relaxation

CHAPTER 12: VIRGO AND PERSONAL DEVELOPMENT

- Structured goal-setting and learning methods
- Self-improvement balanced with realistic steps
- Overcoming self-criticism by focusing on progress

CHAPTER 13: VIRGO COMMUNICATION STYLES

- Direct yet polite conversations
- Detail-focused feedback and active listening
- Adapting to different social or group settings

CHAPTER 14: VIRGO'S RELATIONSHIP WITH FINANCES

- Budgeting, saving, and systematic money handling
- Managing debt, big purchases, and ethical spending
- Blending caution with room for small enjoyments

CHAPTER 15: INTERESTS AND PASTIMES FOR VIRGO

- Hobbies that combine relaxation with practical outcomes
- Enjoyment of learning, crafting, and nature-linked activities
  Need to balance productivity with playful downtime

CHAPTER 16: VIRGOS AND FRIENDSHIP BONDS

- Slow, steady approach to forming close ties
- Reliability and practical help as signs of genuine care
- Managing conflict and respecting personal boundaries

CHAPTER 17: VIRGO AND FAMILY CONNECTIONS

- Roles in parenting, sibling dynamics, or caring for elders
- Organized methods for household tasks and resolving disputes
- Balancing structure with warmth in family life

CHAPTER 18: VIRGO AND SPIRITUAL AWARENESS

- Thoughtful examination of beliefs and traditions
- Connecting practical kindness with moral or faith-based values
- Techniques for calm reflection and inner growth

CHAPTER 19: NOTEWORTHY VIRGO FIGURES

- Examples of public personalities with possible Virgo traits
- Highlights of diligence, precise thinking, and service
- Lessons from their achievements and approaches

CHAPTER 20: THE FUTURE PATH FOR VIRGO

- Adapting steady Virgo values to a changing world
- Using organized habits for modern careers and relationships
- Balancing self-care, flexibility, and compassionate actions

CHAPTER 1: UNDERSTANDING VIRGO'S HISTORY AND SYMBOLISM

Virgo is a special zodiac sign known for its strong connection to helping others and paying close attention to details. Yet, before we talk about the modern ideas about Virgo, it is good to look at where this sign came from. Virgo has a history that goes back thousands of years. People in ancient times looked at the sky and saw patterns of stars. One of these patterns became known as the constellation Virgo. Many different cultures have tried to explain this shape in the night sky, and they shared myths or stories to describe the figure that these stars made.

In the night sky, the constellation Virgo is one of the largest in the zodiac. When we say "zodiac," we mean a group of constellations that the Sun seems to pass through during the year. Long ago, people watched the sky every evening because it helped them keep track of time and seasons. The shape called Virgo has often been seen as a woman, sometimes carrying grain. The reason for the grain is that Virgo has been linked to harvests and abundance. This idea shows how important this constellation was to farming communities a long time ago.

The word "Virgo" itself means "maiden" or "virgin" in Latin. This name highlights a figure often described as pure or untouched. In old stories, the maiden symbol could stand for fresh starts, care, or a special focus on helping life grow. Though the exact image of Virgo changed from place to place, many people agreed on a gentle, caring figure. This figure sometimes showed up as a goddess of the harvest. Sometimes she appeared in other forms. But she was almost always linked with the idea of being kind, tending to the earth, or focusing on making life better.

In ancient Mesopotamia, the area near the Tigris and Euphrates rivers, people already had records of the stars and planets. They looked up at the heavens to guide them in planting crops and choosing dates for important events. We find some of the earliest thoughts about Virgo there. These stories hinted that Virgo was connected to a goddess who cared for the earth. The details varied with each group of people, but the link between Virgo and harvest or farmland remained strong.

In Greek stories, Virgo was sometimes linked to a figure named Demeter, the goddess of agriculture. But Virgo was also connected to another figure named Astraea, a goddess linked to fairness. According to one tale, Astraea was the last immortal to remain on earth during a time when humans had many troubles. She was known for her honesty and her goodness. When people became too unkind, Astraea left the earth and went to the sky, where she became part of the stars. In that story, the constellation Virgo is linked to that idea of fairness and hope.

Over in Rome, people had their own versions of the same idea, since the Romans took many Greek myths and gave them Roman names. So the maiden might be linked to Ceres, the Roman version of Demeter. In other stories, she could be seen as Justitia, the Roman version of Astraea. The link to farming and fairness remained similar. Even if the name changed, the overall meaning stayed much the same: Virgo stood for a gentle, helpful spirit who gave much to the world.

Moving beyond the Mediterranean region, other cultures also recognized Virgo. The Egyptians, for example, had star maps that marked the constellation we now call Virgo, though they saw it in relation to their own gods and spiritual ideas. Everywhere this constellation appeared, people tied it to themes of growth, harvest, or a kind-hearted female figure who guided nature or took care of people. This repeating theme shows that many societies recognized Virgo as a symbol of care and attention to earthly needs.

Later on, astrologers began to write about the traits they believed came from each zodiac sign. They wrote that people born under Virgo might show the same qualities seen in the myths: a tendency to help, a desire to keep things neat, and a careful approach to tasks. This did not mean these traits were proven facts, but they were widely shared as general beliefs. Over time, people kept adding to these ideas, shaping Virgo's image as calm, reasonable, and gentle.

In astrology, Virgo is ruled by the planet Mercury. Mercury is associated with thinking, communication, and quickness. Some astrologers think that because Mercury is the ruler, Virgo tends to be sharp and capable of solving problems in a tidy way. Still, Virgo's link to the element of Earth gives it a down-to-earth nature. This means Virgo is seen as realistic, wanting to see how things work in real life. Combining Mercury's influence and the Earth element often leads people to say Virgo is focused on practical tasks.

The symbol for Virgo is often drawn as an "M" with a small tail curled inside. Some say this shape might stand for three virtues or three important qualities that many hold dear, though the exact meaning can differ across sources. Another idea suggests the "M" shape might link Virgo to Mary, which ties back to certain religious stories. Still, not everyone agrees on the exact origin of this shape. The simplest understanding is that it is an emblem for the maiden or virgin.

When we talk about symbolism, Virgo also appears in art and literature from many periods. Medieval artists sometimes painted a maiden in flowing robes, holding wheat or bread. Writers used Virgo as a symbol to show innocence, wisdom, or the care that a mother figure might show. Over time, these symbols grew stronger. Many see Virgo as a sign that lights the way for growth and improvement, both in nature and in human life.

The historical links to harvest can still be seen. The constellation Virgo appears in the sky in late August and September, a time when many crops are ready for picking in the Northern Hemisphere. This timing made people connect Virgo to success in farming. Farmers believed that the sign's appearance might give them hope for a good yield. People relied on these star patterns because they did not have modern technology to guide them. Instead, they looked for signs in the sky to know when to plant and when to gather their crops.

Virgo's ties to purity do not just mean a literal idea of being untouched. It can also mean a clean spirit or a soul that wants to help. In many older traditions, Virgo's image of a woman with wheat suggests feeding the world or helping it thrive. This idea can be found in many places. It gives a hint about why people sometimes see Virgo as a helpful sign that wants things to be well arranged. These beliefs formed because of the strong link between the constellation and bringing new life from the earth.

Some scholars look at the shape of the constellation Virgo in the night sky and try to find the outline of a woman with wings. They connect that with Astraea, who was said to be a winged goddess. Others see just a lady with an ear of wheat in her hand. The star Spica, which is the brightest star in the constellation Virgo, is said to represent that ear of wheat. Spica is a very bright star and is easy to spot if you look carefully in the southern sky during certain months.

Over time, different languages have changed the name for Virgo. But many languages still keep a word that means "maiden," "young woman," or something similar. This shows how strongly the concept of a youthful, caring figure has stayed with us through the centuries. Even today, there are star charts that mark out Virgo. Astronomers will tell you that it is a large constellation, and it has many galaxies within its boundaries. From a scientific view, there is a cluster of galaxies in that part of the sky called the Virgo Cluster. But that is a topic more for astronomy than astrology.

From an astrological viewpoint, each zodiac sign has a special period when the Sun is in that sign. For Virgo, this usually starts around August 23 and goes through around September 22. During this time, astrologers believe the qualities of Virgo are strong for everyone, but especially for those born under it. Of course, this is a belief system, and many people do not follow it. However, the ancient myths and the repeated stories continue to fascinate many even today.

When we think about Virgo's symbolism, we might notice several main ideas: purity, care, service, and helpfulness. These ideas started with the old stories linking the constellation to goddesses of the harvest or to beings who watched over humans. The shape of a maiden in the sky gave people the impression of a protective figure. Over time, these images became central to how people describe Virgo. Even if you do not believe in astrology, it can be fun to see how ancient myths still shape the way we talk about this star pattern.

Because Virgo is an Earth sign, it is often linked with themes like plants, food, hard work, and nature. That is why the maiden was usually shown with wheat, representing the gifts of the earth. Many who study astrology say that this sign is connected to work that helps others in a practical way, just like the harvest helps feed everyone. In the past, people could not survive without farming. So, having a zodiac sign linked to harvest was a way to thank the heavens for giving them food.

In artwork, the maiden form has sometimes been paired with animals or plants that stand for growth or kindness. We might see Virgo in a painting holding flowers, or guiding children, or looking after a field. These images show the same old idea: Virgo is about making things better and caring for living beings. The constellation's large size might have added to this idea that Virgo is a big and giving presence in the sky, shining down with bright stars.

Many astrologers and historians note how Virgo's history blends different cultures. Some parts come from Babylonian roots, some from Greek myths, some from Roman stories, and others from local legends all over the world. Yet, all these different tales point to a figure who stands for goodness, honesty, and the quest to bring help to others. This is what keeps Virgo's story alive even today. People want to hold on to symbols that remind them of helpful qualities.

As we think about Virgo's history, we see that it grew from people looking at the sky and feeling wonder. This constellation stood out because of its bright star, Spica, and because of how it rises in the months of late summer. Farmers paid attention to it. Storytellers created tales about it. Then astrologers added more layers, linking it to Mercury and Earth. Each step of this process changed Virgo's image slightly, but the core idea remained a maiden who watched over harvests and gave care to those in need.

Today, many people do not rely on stars to tell them when to plant or harvest. We have new tools. But the interest in astrology continues in modern life. Some see Virgo as an important sign because it represents kindness, neatness, and caution. Others might not follow astrology but can still enjoy the rich stories. The symbol of a gentle helper is something that has always been welcome in human culture.

Virgo's place in art, myths, and star lore reminds us of how ancient people explained the sky. They did not have telescopes like we do. Instead, they looked up and formed shapes out of patterns of light. They connected those shapes to the world around them. Virgo's link to farmland is just one example of how our ancestors made sense of nature. Their stories about a caring figure or a fair goddess let them feel safe and guided by a higher power. Whether or not we believe in these myths, it can be interesting to learn about the roots of these beliefs.

In summary, Virgo's history is long and varied. People from many regions took this cluster of stars and turned it into a symbol of nurturing or support. The Latin name, meaning "maiden," stuck around through centuries. The idea of a woman holding wheat or representing helpful acts carried on. Today, we still see Virgo in horoscopes, works of art, and even in modern entertainment. Its symbolism remains tied to kind acts, realism, and a sense of purity that comes from a wish to do good.

CHAPTER 2: TYPICAL VIRGO PERSONALITY TRAITS

When people talk about Virgo personality traits, they often mention a calm, caring, and organized manner. Because Virgo is often linked to service and practicality, many believe that those born under this sign pay great attention to details in everything they do. Some might say this is because Virgo is ruled by the planet Mercury. Mercury is connected to thinking and speaking, which may make Virgo individuals good at analyzing situations or explaining ideas clearly.

One quality often linked to Virgo is a desire for neatness. This can show up as keeping a tidy desk, arranging items in a drawer, or making sure every detail in a plan is correct. Virgos may not like chaos. They often seek to create order in their surroundings because it helps them feel more at ease. Even though not every Virgo is a neat person, many find comfort in having clear methods for doing things.

Another common trait for Virgo is being helpful. Many feel that Virgos like to assist others, whether by offering a thoughtful tip or stepping in to support a friend who is feeling overwhelmed. This desire to be of use can come from a caring heart. Some say that because Virgo is an Earth sign, it is grounded in real-world actions, which makes Virgos want to be practical helpers. Rather than just talking, they often show their care by fixing something, giving advice, or solving a problem.

Virgos are sometimes described as perfectionists. This means they may try very hard to do tasks without mistakes. They might review things more than once to ensure everything is correct. While this can be a strength, it can also cause stress if Virgos become too strict with themselves or others. Some Virgos learn to handle this by reminding themselves that nobody is perfect. They try to see small mistakes as normal parts of being human.

Being a thinker is another Virgo trait. People often notice that Virgos like to process information and are eager to learn new things. This can make them great at research or planning. If you see a Virgo studying something, they might spend a lot of time reading about it and writing down details. Their love for understanding everything thoroughly can be a big advantage in many fields, from science to creative projects.

On the emotional side, Virgos might appear cautious. They could be slow to trust because they want to be sure about a person's intentions. Some might say this is because Virgos do not like being vulnerable without reason. However, once they do trust someone, they can be very loyal and show a lot of kindness. This loyalty can make them wonderful friends who stick by your side.

Virgos are also known for noticing the little things that others might miss. They have an eye for picking out errors in writing, small flaws in a design, or a slight change in someone's behavior. This can make them seem picky, but it can also be very useful. For example, if a Virgo is working on a school project or a job assignment, they might catch problems early and fix them before they grow bigger.

Because of their detail-focused nature, some Virgos can be hard on themselves. They might worry if they do not do well in a test or if they feel they have made a mistake. It can be helpful for them to remember that learning takes time and everyone slips up sometimes. Some Virgos manage this self-criticism by setting realistic goals and rewarding themselves for each step they complete.

Virgos often show a sense of responsibility. If they say they will do something, they try to follow through. This can make them dependable friends and family members. Others might come to see them as reliable, the kind of person you can count on to pick you up on time or to do their share of the work. This sense of duty is part of their earth element side, which encourages them to be steady and consistent.

Some people say Virgos can be shy. They may not always jump into social settings, preferring instead to watch from a distance before taking part. This is not always true, but it is a common description. Even those who are more outgoing might still have a reflective side, wanting to think before they speak. This can be good because they often speak with clarity once they are ready.

Kindness is another trait often linked to Virgo. People may find them caring, especially if you share a concern. A Virgo may want to solve the issue rather than just talk about it. They often prefer to do something practical. So, if you are sad, a Virgo might offer to help by doing a chore or running an errand, rather than simply offering words of comfort. This action-focused kindness is one of the hallmarks of the sign.

Their planet ruler Mercury can also show up in Virgo's fondness for communication, but in a careful way. While some signs ruled by Mercury may like talking a lot, Virgos may be more precise and thoughtful. They can be good listeners, and they might remember small details you mention. Some people are surprised when a Virgo recalls something said weeks earlier. This can make Virgos helpful in group tasks, as they often keep track of points or instructions others forget.

Virgos can also have a desire for learning new skills. This can turn them into students who enjoy reading, or adults who sign up for classes on different topics. Many Virgos are self-starters who like to figure things out on their own. They might watch tutorials, read manuals, or experiment in a quiet way until they perfect the skill. Because they are patient with the learning process, they can become quite good at tasks that require focus.

At times, Virgos may need to remember not to become overly critical. Because they often see how something can be improved, they might share these thoughts with others, even when others do not ask. This can cause misunderstandings. For example, a Virgo might point out a friend's small mistake just to be helpful. But the friend might feel that the Virgo is being too picky. Learning how to kindly offer feedback is an important lesson for many Virgos.

In groups, Virgos can be the ones who organize everything. For instance, if there is a class project, a Virgo might make a clear plan of who does what. They might also set up a schedule for finishing each part. This can help the group do well. Some Virgos love this kind of role because it uses their strengths in planning and efficiency. However, they might also need to learn to be flexible if others have different ideas.

Virgos are sometimes associated with modesty. They might not brag about their achievements, even if they have done something impressive. Instead, they focus on what is left to be done or what can be better next time. This humble approach can be nice, but it might lead to not giving themselves enough credit for their hard work. Friends might need to remind a Virgo to pause and feel good about their progress.

Many Virgos value honesty. They tend to feel uneasy if they sense someone is not telling the truth. Since they appreciate facts and clear thinking, they may not like grand claims without evidence. This desire for honesty can make them direct, though not always in a harsh way. They just see little point in going around the main issue.

Still, they usually try to be respectful when pointing out what they think is correct or incorrect.

Virgos can have a strong sense of well-being. Because they pay attention to details, they might be aware of their health and daily habits. Some enjoy making sure they eat balanced meals or get regular exercise. They might also be careful about cleanliness, like washing hands often or keeping their workspace free from clutter. This is not about perfection but rather about feeling good by keeping up healthy routines.

At times, Virgos might worry more than other signs. They can think about different possibilities and consider what might go wrong. While this can help them be ready, it can also cause stress if they fixate too much on negative outcomes. Finding ways to stay calm, such as simple breathing exercises or hobbies, can help a Virgo feel balanced. This also lets them use their planning skills to find good solutions instead of just worrying.

Virgos often get along well with people who value honesty, structure, and mutual support. They might clash with those who are overly messy or do not take tasks seriously. However, because Virgos can adapt, they can learn to manage different personalities if given time. Over the years, many Virgos discover that it is okay if others have different work styles. They can still share what they are good at without expecting everyone to be as organized as they are.

In friendships, Virgos are usually very supportive. They might check in on their friends' well-being and show concern if something seems off. Since they are keen observers, they might notice small changes in a friend's mood or actions. This can be a comfort for friends who need someone to pay attention and care. However, Virgos should also remember that not everyone wants help all the time, so they must respect boundaries as well.

When it comes to making decisions, Virgos tend to gather information first. They might research or list pros and cons. This can be good because it makes them less likely to rush. But sometimes they might overthink, worrying about every little possibility. Striking a balance is key. Many Virgos learn to trust their instincts more as they grow, though they still like having facts before making final choices.

Some Virgos enjoy creative tasks, but they will often do them in a structured way. For example, a Virgo artist might plan a painting in detail before putting brush to canvas. A Virgo writer might make a thorough outline before starting the story. This can lead to work that is polished and well-thought-out. Their desire for neatness and order can show up in their creative pieces, sometimes giving them a style that is both pretty and precise.

In summary, Virgo personalities are often described as gentle, caring, and tidy. They notice small details, like to help, and seek to do tasks well. Their link to Mercury adds a thoughtful quality, while their Earth element keeps them focused on real-life concerns. At times, they might be too tough on themselves or too worried about small flaws. However, they also have a positive side of being dependable, honest, and supportive to friends and family. Recognizing these traits can help Virgos find balance, allowing them to use their special gifts in a way that helps both themselves and others.

CHAPTER 3: VIRGO IN ANCIENT STORIES AND LEGENDS

In many old tales, the constellation Virgo took on different names and faces. Ancient observers of the sky often created stories to explain the patterns of stars. They saw figures in the heavens that connected to daily life and important values. Virgo, shaped like a maiden, became one of these major figures. Around the world, people shared myths that linked Virgo to a helpful or wise goddess. These stories often focused on nature, kindness, and looking after people in need.

Among the Greeks, Virgo was sometimes linked to a figure named Astraea. Ancient texts describe Astraea as a shining example of goodness. She lived among humans at first. The myths say that in the early days, humans were honest and peaceful, so Astraea stayed on earth. Over time, people grew more selfish and angry with each other. Seeing this, Astraea felt sad and chose to leave. She rose into the sky, becoming part of the stars. Some stories say that the constellation Virgo represents Astraea watching from above.

Greek storytellers also connected Virgo to Demeter, the goddess of grains and farmland. Demeter cared greatly for her daughter, Persephone, and for the success of crops. Some versions suggest that the maiden image in the constellation mirrors Demeter's role, holding wheat to show her link with harvest time. The sign of Virgo appears in the sky around late summer in the Northern Hemisphere, the season when fields can be full of crops. Though modern accounts differ, Demeter often stands out as an important motherly figure in Greek tradition.

To the Romans, many Greek tales seemed similar to their own. They had a goddess named Ceres, who was nearly the same figure as Demeter. Ceres watched over farming, making sure there was food for the people. Ancient Romans held various events to honor her. They told stories of a caring goddess who guided the growth of plants. When they looked at the sky and noticed the maiden of Virgo, they often thought of Ceres and the idea of plenty for everyone.

Alongside Ceres, the Romans also liked the idea of Justitia, or the spirit of fairness. In some versions, Astraea and Justitia merged. The maiden in the sky could show both the caring side of the harvest and the wish for fairness in human dealings. Some coins and statues from ancient Rome show a female figure holding scales, symbolizing balance. While that image is more directly linked to Libra, Roman stories sometimes connected the virtues of honesty and justice with the constellation Virgo as well.

Outside of the Mediterranean area, the constellation Virgo also appeared in the tales of Mesopotamia. This region covered lands around the Tigris and Euphrates Rivers, such as Babylon and Assyria. The people there were among the first to map the stars for daily use. Some mention a goddess named Shala who held a stalk of grain. She was seen as watching over farmland and weather. Scholars suggest that this figure might have been linked to what we now call Virgo. These ancient myths often included strong female deities who provided vital resources to the land.

In other Mesopotamian myths, we hear of Ishtar or Inanna, powerful goddesses who ruled many aspects of life, including love and harvest. Although the exact match to Virgo can be debated, many stories hint at female figures who hold important keys to nature and growth. Over time, as star lore traveled, certain traits from one region's goddess might blend with another. This is why we see repeated themes of a helpful maiden with a link to farmland or moral goodness.

In Egypt, some star maps also recognized a group of stars that match the constellation Virgo. While the Egyptians had their own names for these stars, the idea of a female presence in that part of the sky was not unusual. Their myths often centered on strong goddesses, such as Isis, though it is not always certain which goddess lined up exactly with Virgo. Still, the link between fertile farmland along the Nile and the bright stars overhead showed up in many Egyptian rituals. They saw the sky as guiding and protecting life on earth.

Historians have found that early cultures often connected constellations with the harvest because the timing of the stars' visibility matched seasons for planting and gathering crops. Virgo's shape and the presence of the bright star Spica (which can be translated in Latin to "ear of grain") added to this idea. Farmers would watch for Spica as a sign related to certain months. Because food was vital, it made sense that one of the biggest constellations would represent a kind giver of wheat or other crops.

Moving further east, in parts of ancient India, star watchers had elaborate charts that included a form of the constellation Virgo. Indian astrology, or Jyotisha, placed importance on the lunar mansions, which are segments of the sky for the Moon's path. Though not exactly the same as Western zodiac signs, some areas overlapped. A part of the Indian sky lore featured a maiden form. Because India also placed great importance on farmland and the yearly monsoons, the notion of a caring feminine figure in the sky was fairly common.

In China, star maps had different groupings of stars called "mansions" and "constellations." The set of stars that Western astronomers call Virgo might have been split into more than one figure in the Chinese tradition. Still, there are legends that speak of weaving maidens or other female figures in the heavens. While these stories do not match the Western concept of Virgo exactly, the idea of a young female presence in the sky reappears. Cultures that farmed widely often passed down stories about women who brought blessings to the fields.

Around the globe, from northern lands to tropical zones, people recognized that certain constellations rose during certain times of the year. They gave them symbolic roles in their myths. Virgo's large size and bright star made it stand out. The connection to the harvest or a helpful goddess was often repeated because having enough food was a major concern for early societies. People wanted to believe a kindly spirit watched over their crops and well-being.

Some of these stories also connect Virgo with events or legends about plenty or moral values. In places where the sign was linked to justice, like in the story of Astraea, the maiden's departure from earth highlighted a time when humans no longer lived in harmony. This theme appears in multiple cultures: a good goddess or spirit leaves when humans turn away from truth or order. The constellation thus became a reminder that goodness still exists, though it may be out of direct reach.

In certain Greek stories, this link between Virgo and moral themes extends to a golden age of humankind. The poet Hesiod wrote of different ages, starting with a golden age when gods and mortals lived closer. As ages progressed, people lost their innocence. Astraea's exit to the sky marked the final step before the gods fully removed themselves. Even though this story is quite old, it shows how humans used the stars to reflect on the changes in their own society.

Other legends connect Virgo to wise women or oracles. Because Virgo was linked to Mercury (the planet of thought and communication) in later astrology, some believed that the maiden could bring messages or warnings to mortals. These smaller tales might not be as famous as the big stories of Demeter or Astraea, but they still show the variety of roles that the Virgo constellation could play in legends. At times, she was a gentle farmer's helper. At other times, she was a beacon of fairness or a messenger of wisdom.

In many paintings and sculptures from older times, artists portrayed Virgo as a woman dressed in flowing garments, often with wheat in her hand. This imagery might come from the Greek or Roman harvest goddess concept, or from local forms of the maiden story. Over the centuries, the art changed styles, yet the same basic picture remained: a serene figure who stands for caring, kindness, and the prosperity of the land. It was a way to pass on the myth to younger generations who might not read the old texts.

Some cultures saw the constellation as a figure of pure or original goodness. This idea of purity did not always mean an absence of flaws. Rather, it suggested an honest, unspoiled desire to help or guide the world. People liked to see a protective figure up among the stars. In times when life was uncertain, they could look to Virgo and think of a motherly presence or a guardian who wanted them to find the right path. This comfort was part of how star myths helped people cope with daily struggles.

Along with the bright star Spica, Virgo contains other stars that formed parts of different myths. For example, some cultures named individual stars after their own local heroes or animals. But the overall shape of a maiden remained quite common. Ancient star catalogs from astronomers like Ptolemy also noted Virgo as one of the zodiac constellations. Ptolemy's work influenced astrology for centuries, as it provided details about where each constellation sat in relation to others.

One interesting detail about the old stories is how they mixed farming with moral lessons. For example, if Virgo represented a harvest goddess, it reminded people of the need to work the fields carefully to get good results. If Virgo showed a figure of fairness, it reminded people to be decent toward each other. The stars were not just pretty lights; they were pointers to values that ancient societies held important. Because Virgo was large and visible, she served as a strong symbol for these lessons.

In some versions of Mesopotamian legend, the figure linked to Virgo also protected water sources and the weather. This was crucial, since the right amount of rain in the right season meant a good yield. A caring goddess who oversaw such matters would be held in high esteem. People might have prayed or made offerings, hoping that the goddess in the sky would keep the balance of nature. Even though these actions differ from modern viewpoints, they show how serious and practical stargazing was in the past.

The Roman writer Virgil mentioned the star Spica in some of his poems, connecting it to the fields of grain. In Latin, spica can mean a head of wheat, which fits with how artists drew Virgo carrying wheat. This detail deepened the bond between the constellation and farmland. Readers of Virgil's works might have looked at the sky, recognized Spica, and thought of the promise of a fruitful harvest. Such poetry gave a cultural richness to the star stories, linking them to everyday life.

In medieval Europe, many star charts included Virgo with the label "Virgo, the Virgin," in Latin. Monks and scholars copied these charts, passing along earlier Greek and Roman knowledge. Though the old polytheistic beliefs were replaced by newer faiths, the shape in the sky and its classical name stayed. Over time, different Christian writers gave Virgo new meanings, sometimes connecting the constellation to religious figures of purity. Yet the classical idea of the wheat-carrying maiden also survived in texts about the zodiac.

Even in regions like northern Europe, which had shorter growing seasons, star lore that came from the Mediterranean took hold. Vikings, Celts, and others had their own sets of myths, but after contact with the Roman world, they also learned about the zodiac signs. The figure of Virgo might not have been as prominent in their older myths, yet it became a part of later sky lore. This shows how stories can travel across borders and weave together over time.

Although many of these legends differ in details, the concept of a caring female figure remains strong. Sometimes, she is a goddess who stands for farmland. Sometimes, she is a spirit of fairness. In every case, Virgo is portrayed with a sense of goodness and watchfulness. That common theme has kept the constellation special through many centuries. Even today, if you look at a star map, you might see the drawn outline of a maiden. You are seeing the same shape that made people of ancient days spin tales of warmth and hope.

In this way, Virgo serves as a link between myths from far-reaching cultures. She embodies harvest, honesty, and often a gentleness that resonates with human wishes for a safer world. These stories offered guidance in earlier times, whether teaching moral lessons or showing when to plant seeds. Though our modern understanding of astronomy has changed, the myths keep their charm. They connect us to a time when people gazed at the night sky and found not just stars, but moral examples and helpful symbols.

CHAPTER 4: VIRGO'S ELEMENT AND ITS INFLUENCE

In astrology, each zodiac sign is connected to one of four elements: Earth, Air, Fire, or Water. Virgo belongs to the Earth element. This element is often linked to stability, practical thinking, and a focus on concrete results. When people hear "Earth sign," they usually think of individuals who like to see real progress in their tasks. They may also connect Earth signs with being grounded, because earth is the ground beneath our feet, giving us a strong base.

For Virgo, being an Earth sign means focusing on details in daily life. This can show up in how Virgos work hard to get tasks done carefully. Because they often want to produce real outcomes, they can excel in tasks that need precise methods. Earth energy supports an interest in tidiness, planning, and problem-solving. This side of Virgo often appears when they make schedules, organize items, or set firm goals to complete a project.

Earth signs are sometimes seen as steady companions. Taurus and Capricorn are the other Earth signs, and all three share a preference for practical approaches. Yet, Virgo stands out because it is also ruled by Mercury, which adds a mental sharpness. Virgo's Earth quality merges with Mercury's emphasis on thinking. So, rather than simply working hard in a physical way, Virgo tends to approach tasks with a method that includes research, writing, or logical steps.

The Earth element in Virgo can also lead to a wish for security. Many Virgos like to feel sure about their finances, their living space, and their future plans. They might set up clear budgets, research job options carefully, or keep track of small changes in their environment. This does not mean Virgos must be wealthy to be happy, but they like to know they have a firm base to rely on. That sense of stability can give them peace of mind.

Practical thinking is often a hallmark of Earth signs, and Virgo is no exception. If a problem arises, Virgo might break it down into smaller parts to see what is going on. For instance, if a machine is not working, a Virgo might follow each step to find the cause. This approach can make them good at repairs or at least at identifying errors. They aim to ground their thinking in facts, avoiding guesses whenever possible.

Because Virgo is connected to the Earth element, nature might play a calming role for them. Many Virgos enjoy spending time outdoors, taking walks, or gardening. Seeing plants grow or tending to animals can soothe the mind of someone with strong Earth energy. This does not mean every Virgo is a lover of the outdoors. Still, many find that close contact with nature helps them relax. It fits their overall sense of wanting to be in touch with the real world.

Earth signs often have a careful way of moving through changes. Instead of jumping into a big decision, Virgo might test the waters bit by bit. They look at the situation from different angles, collecting facts. Once they feel things are in order, they will move forward. This can sometimes appear to be cautious, but it also helps Virgos avoid large mistakes. It is a methodical style that works well in areas where details matter.

Another effect of the Earth element is the desire for tangibility. Virgos might want to see the results of their work clearly. For example, if they are learning a new skill, they like to produce something they can hold, read, or at least measure. If their efforts remain entirely abstract, they might feel uneasy. So they tend to lean toward tasks or hobbies where they can say, "I made this," or "I improved that," and see the proof.

Virgos can also use Earth energy to stay calm under stress. When faced with a tense situation, they might focus on practical steps that can fix the issue. Instead of panicking, they could list items that need addressing and tackle them one by one. This down-to-earth approach can be comforting for others who feel overwhelmed. In group settings, a Virgo might offer helpful methods, reminding everyone to keep their feet on solid ground.

Sometimes, Earth energy can cause a person to feel stuck if they worry too much about making everything perfect. Virgos might fall into this trap because their attention to detail can make them hesitant. They may want absolute certainty before moving on. Learning to trust their instincts, combined with careful planning, can help Virgos avoid overthinking. When they find the right balance, the Earth element becomes a reliable power that allows them to reach their goals.

This element also shapes Virgo's way of expressing love or care. Instead of big shows of affection, an Earth-aligned sign might prefer consistent support. For example, a Virgo might help a friend fix a computer or organize a schedule if that friend seems lost. These actions are a solid way of showing care, even if they do not come with fancy words. This reliability is something many people appreciate about Earth signs in general.

Virgo's Earth nature can also show up in their moral values. They might believe in being truthful and in acting ethically. Because the Earth element is about solidity and what is real, Virgos might feel uneasy around dishonesty or trickery. They prefer clear rules. Some Virgos take this further and become advocates for fair treatment in everyday life. They believe in practical goodness, such as being on time or keeping promises.

Comparing Earth signs with Air signs can highlight differences. Air signs (like Gemini, Libra, Aquarius) often enjoy ideas and talking, possibly jumping from one thought to another. Virgos, on the other hand, prefer to tie ideas to concrete plans. They may talk about a topic, but they usually want to apply the ideas in a real sense. While Air signs handle theory well, Earth signs want to see how theory works in daily tasks.

Comparing Earth signs with Fire signs (like Aries, Leo, Sagittarius) also reveals interesting contrasts. Fire signs often move quickly, guided by strong enthusiasm. Earth signs tend to move at a steadier pace, double-checking each step. A Virgo might see a Fire sign as too impulsive at times. Meanwhile, a Fire sign might find Virgo overly cautious. Still, if they work together, they can balance each other out, with one supplying excitement and the other providing structure.

When compared to Water signs (Cancer, Scorpio, Pisces), Earth signs might appear more level-headed. Water signs often rely on feelings, while Earth signs rely on facts. A Virgo might think, "Let's fix the problem with a plan," while a Water sign could think, "Let's first understand everyone's emotions." Both sides are useful. A Virgo can learn to value emotional insight from Water signs, and Water signs can benefit from Virgo's methodical problem-solving.

Another notable aspect of the Earth element is endurance. This can be seen when Virgo decides to master a skill or complete a major goal. They may stick with a task even if it is dull, because they see the importance of finishing. This trait can help them handle jobs that others might give up on. They find satisfaction in taking something from start to finish, knowing they did each step properly.

Virgos sometimes bring this same Earthy steadiness into relationships. They might not rush into a bond, but once they commit, they aim to be loyal. This can give friends and loved ones a sense of trust. They know the Virgo in their life will try hard to keep promises. However, Virgos also want their own space to think and handle tasks. This is not because they dislike company, but because they often need quiet time to feel in balance.

On a day-to-day level, Virgo's Earth energy can show up in how they handle chores or personal projects. They might enjoy having a routine, like setting up a weekly plan for grocery shopping or cleaning. A schedule can help them feel stable. While other signs might find routines dull, Virgos often find they reduce stress. Knowing what needs to be done each day can be comforting.

Virgos also tend to be mindful of health, which aligns with the Earth element's link to the body and natural living. Some Virgos try to eat well, choosing foods that make them feel energetic rather than bogged down. They may also pay attention to hygiene, making sure their environment is neat. This does not require perfection, but it is part of their desire for a clean, calm setting that supports well-being.

Because Earth energy can be quite grounded, Virgos might not always connect with abstract or spiritual concepts right away. That does not mean they cannot be spiritual; it just means they often want practical proof or results in any system they follow. They might study different ideas or philosophies but choose to apply them in daily life. This approach keeps them rooted, though it can also limit them if they do not allow room for the unknown.

In work environments, Virgo's Earth qualities can be a big advantage. They might excel in roles that need attention to detail, such as research, organization, or editing. Their skill in carefully checking information can prevent errors. Because they like being useful, they might be drawn to fields that let them help others in a direct way—perhaps in healthcare or service fields. This satisfies their Earthy need to do practical good.

On the downside, too much Earth energy could make a Virgo seem rigid. They might insist on following a plan to the letter, even when changes might be beneficial. If a coworker or family member suggests a new approach, a Virgo might initially resist unless they see the evidence that it will succeed. Learning to adapt without losing stability is a useful skill. Many Virgos pick this up over time, finding a healthy blend of reliability and openness.

In personal growth, Virgos might rely on Earth energy to set realistic steps. If they want to improve a skill, they outline the sub-steps and track their progress. This methodical way usually works well, as long as they do not push themselves too hard. Small achievements can add up, giving them confidence. The Earth element helps them see that solid improvement can happen bit by bit, leading to steady results rather than big leaps that might not last.

Earth signs in general are often described as builders, each in their own way. For Virgo, this might mean building methods or procedures that help people or organizations run more smoothly. It might mean guiding others to be more organized. It could also mean creating a sense of safety at home by arranging things in a neat, welcoming way. This building nature is less about constructing physical buildings and more about creating order and support.

In conclusion, Virgo's Earth element is a key force behind its traits. It shapes the sign's stable nature, love of practical tasks, and steady pursuit of goals. It also contributes to a caring style that shows through hands-on help rather than flashy displays. Paired with Mercury's influence, Virgo's Earth side supports a smart, clear, and thorough way of living. By understanding how the Earth element works, Virgos can use their grounded qualities to make a positive impact, both for themselves and for those around them.

CHAPTER 5: STRENGTHS THAT SHAPE THE VIRGO CHARACTER

When people talk about Virgo, they often mention qualities like neatness or being organized. Yet, there is much more to Virgo's strong points than these simple traits. Virgos can show many forms of quiet ability and kindness that may not be obvious at first. Below, we explore some of the key strengths that many Virgos might have. Each quality can shine differently in every individual, so not all Virgos will show these traits in the exact same way. Still, these strengths often appear in those born under this sign.

Attentiveness to Details

A strong trait that many Virgos show is an ability to notice small points. When they look at a paper, a work project, or a set of instructions, they often spot things that others overlook. This can be a huge help in many tasks. For example, if a Virgo is preparing a meal, they might pay special attention to the exact amounts of each ingredient. This leads to a recipe that turns out just right.

In professional settings, a Virgo's detail-focused approach can save a group from major mistakes. If they are in charge of reviewing documents, they might pick up on typing errors, small calculation issues, or unclear phrases. Because of this, friends or coworkers might trust a Virgo's opinions when it comes to refining plans. This power of spotting little things helps keep them and their team on track.

At the same time, being so detail-oriented can bring delight in creative fields. A Virgo artist might focus on subtle shading in a painting, or a Virgo musician might carefully adjust each note until it sounds perfect. This precision often serves as a hidden strength, allowing them to produce polished work that stands out.

Steadfast Reliability

Virgos often show strong dependability. They tend to keep promises and meet deadlines. This does not mean every Virgo is perfect at being on time, but many hold themselves to high standards of responsibility. In group tasks, a Virgo might be the person who says, "I will handle this part," and then follows through without fail.

This sense of reliability makes Virgos valuable friends as well. If someone close to them is going through a hard time, a Virgo might be the one to show up and quietly help. They might do tasks like running errands, organizing a messy area, or making sure forms are filled out properly. Their calm and steady way of offering assistance can help others relax, knowing things are under control.

Being reliable also means Virgos often think ahead. They do not want to leave things until the last moment. If they have an important responsibility, they usually plan well. This practical mindset is linked to their Earth element, which favors stability and firm ground. By preparing early, they help reduce stress for themselves and for the people around them.

Willingness to Learn and Improve

While some signs might rely on sheer confidence or quick action, Virgos often believe in gradually mastering a subject. They might devote hours to reading or practicing, making sure they understand the basics before moving on. This steady learning curve becomes a strength because it creates a strong foundation.

If a Virgo becomes interested in gardening, for instance, they might read books about soil and plant care. Then they would try planting a small patch, observing how each seed grows, and taking careful notes on what works. Over time, this methodical approach can lead to impressive results, such as a garden that thrives.

The same applies to other skills, whether it is cooking, coding, writing, or crafting. Virgos' focus on self-improvement helps them become quite capable in areas they choose to explore. They might not brag about what they learn, but they quietly gather knowledge and apply it in practical ways.

Observant and Thoughtful Support

Many Virgos are thoughtful about what others need. Because they pay attention to small signs, they might notice when a friend is feeling a bit down or struggling with a task. They may sense that a friend who usually smiles is quieter than usual, or that someone's posture looks tense. This ability to pick up on hints can help them provide support at just the right time.

When a Virgo decides to help, they usually do it in a gentle and grounded way. Instead of grand gestures, they might handle little tasks that make life easier. They could tidy a kitchen, provide well-researched answers to a question, or offer tools that solve a practical problem. This type of caring can be very comforting, because it addresses real concerns rather than just speaking about them.

Some friends might say Virgos are their "go-to" people when they need honest advice. A Virgo often listens carefully, takes in all the information, and then shares a reasoned view. Even if they do not have an immediate fix, just having someone who thoroughly hears them out can help others feel better.

Calm Problem-Solving Approach

One notable strength of Virgo is the ability to stay calm when faced with an issue. Rather than panicking, Virgos often try to break the problem down step by step. They gather details, consider possible options, and then choose a path that seems most logical. This can be reassuring for others who might be stressed or uncertain.

For example, imagine a group project where something goes wrong, like files getting lost on a computer. Some group members might become upset, but a Virgo could say, "Let's see if they are in the backup folder," or "Maybe we can reconstruct them with older versions." This clear-headed approach keeps everyone moving toward a solution.

Because they value careful steps, Virgos also tend to learn from mistakes. Instead of dwelling on what went wrong, they gather lessons on how to prevent it next time. This mindset can help them improve over the long run, building up knowledge that makes them ever more efficient in handling surprises.

Helpful Resource Management

Virgos can be quite clever in how they use resources, such as time, money, and materials. They do not always believe in throwing money at a problem. Instead, they might look for ways to fix or reuse items. This practical thinking helps them save money and reduce waste.

If a Virgo wants to start a new hobby but does not want to spend too much, they might look for used equipment or try borrowing first. If they see they enjoy the hobby, they will invest more. This thoughtful way of handling money can also apply to bigger goals, such as planning for education, running a household, or assisting family members who might need financial advice.

Time management is another area where Virgos can shine. They often schedule tasks carefully, breaking big projects into smaller steps. They might create simple charts or lists, making sure each deadline is clear. This system helps them avoid feeling swamped by last-minute work. It also shows that they value each minute and do not like to waste effort.

Sense of Humility

While some people might flaunt their abilities, many Virgos show a more modest side. They prefer letting their work speak for itself instead of drawing attention to their successes. This humility can be refreshing in a world that often praises showy behavior.

When a Virgo completes a complex project, they might say, "I just followed the steps I planned." They may not realize how impressive their accomplishment is. Others see the value in their quiet dedication, but Virgos might shrug it off and think there is still room to improve. This down-to-earth view can make them approachable.

Humility can also mean that Virgos treat others with kindness, regardless of status. They might speak politely to people from all walks of life, showing the same respect to a shop clerk as they do to a CEO. This approach fosters goodwill and can help them form steady connections wherever they go.

Eagerness to Refine and Upgrade

Virgos often like to tinker with processes, seeing if something can be made better. If a system is in place at work or at home, a Virgo might say, "How about we adjust this part so it flows more smoothly?" They do not see re-checking or improving as a chore. Instead, they see it as a positive challenge.

This drive to refine can appear in tasks like cooking, where a Virgo might try slightly different spices each time to find the perfect flavor. It can also show up in job settings, like in an office, where they might design new forms that speed up workflow. Their desire to optimize can be a big plus for any team aiming to run more efficiently.

Sometimes, this same quality can spill into personal habits. A Virgo might track their exercise routine, noting which days are best for a certain activity. Then they tweak their schedule based on what they learn. Over time, they might discover which patterns bring the best results. This love of refining helps them constantly make small but important gains in many areas of life.

Deep Sense of Care for Well-Being

Virgos often have a strong drive to maintain well-being for themselves and for others. This might mean eating foods that provide long-lasting energy, staying hydrated, and choosing balanced meals. Some might have a knack for reading about health topics, comparing tips, and testing out small changes.

Their care for well-being can also lead them to share information with friends, such as an easy recipe or an exercise tip. They usually do it in a calm way, saying, "This is what worked for me," rather than pushing anyone too hard. If someone is in poor health, a Virgo might help by suggesting realistic steps or walking them through new routines.

In addition, Virgos might think carefully about their mental and emotional health. They could keep a simple journal to track moods or events, looking for patterns that bring joy or stress. Because they love to analyze details, they can discover small things that affect how they feel. This awareness can eventually help them shape habits that lead to more balanced emotions.

Patience in Building Skills

Another key strength for Virgos is patience in skill-building. They realize that quick fixes might not lead to deep knowledge. When they pick up something like playing a musical instrument, they recognize it takes time to learn the basics. They are willing to practice each day, even if the improvement seems slow.

This trait can apply to academic subjects too. If a Virgo struggles with math, they might stay after class or spend extra hours reviewing formulas. They have trust in the process of gradual learning. In the end, they often achieve a solid understanding that sticks with them for a long time.

Patience can also help them in group efforts. Instead of pushing someone who is learning at a different pace, a Virgo might calmly explain things step by step. This makes them good tutors or mentors, especially for those who feel shy about asking questions. Their steady approach ensures that real progress happens without unnecessary pressure.

Skill in Practical Communication

Because Virgo is ruled by Mercury, there is often a knack for communication. But unlike other Mercury-led signs, Virgo's style is more practical. They do not always speak for the sake of speaking; they speak when they have something useful to share.

Virgos might also excel at writing down instructions or guidelines that are easy to follow. Whether it is writing out directions for a friend or creating a manual at work, they tend to be clear and organized. People receiving these instructions usually appreciate how logical and straightforward they are.

At times, this communication style means Virgos might focus on facts and real-world examples. They may prefer showing how something works through steps rather than talking about theories. This can be especially helpful in jobs that call for training new team members or building lessons in a classroom.

Resourceful Planning

One of Virgo's biggest strengths is resourceful planning. They do not just set goals, but also figure out how to reach them step by step. If they decide to learn a language, for instance, they might list helpful materials, plan daily lessons, track their progress, and make notes of tricky parts.

This careful method can extend to financial goals. If a Virgo wants to save for something important, they might create a basic chart of expenses and see where they can cut back. They might read about money-saving tips, compare options, and put their plan into action. Over time, their methodical approach can lead to big achievements.

Virgos might also assist family or friends in planning. If a relative wants to organize a family event, a Virgo might step in with a workable schedule, a shopping list, and a plan for who does what. This ability to break down tasks into clear actions is part of their Earth element nature, keeping things firmly grounded.

Quiet Leadership

While not every Virgo seeks a leadership role, some show a natural capacity for it, especially in settings where organization is key. Their calm presence and careful approach can make them effective leaders who keep the group on task. They may not raise their voice, but they earn respect by being consistent and fair.

In these roles, Virgos usually set clear expectations. They give constructive feedback and try to show the best way to handle tasks rather than simply commanding people around. Because they value steadiness, they often avoid sudden changes, preferring to make sure everyone understands updates step by step.

When challenges arise, a Virgo leader might say, "Let's gather the facts and make a plan." This straightforward response can help a team remain calm and productive. Over time, people often learn they can trust a Virgo leader to see them through tricky situations without too much fuss.

Empathy Expressed in Real Actions

Virgos may not always show big emotional displays, but they often express empathy through what they do. This is different from some other signs that might rely on dramatic gestures. With Virgo, you might see empathy in the way they quietly ensure someone has what they need.

For example, if a coworker is swamped, a Virgo might offer to handle a few tasks. If a friend is upset, a Virgo could give them a neat, calming environment to rest in or offer a small meal. They might check on someone by sending a simple message that says, "I'm here if you need me."

This genuine care can be especially touching. It shows that Virgos do not just feel for people; they act in helpful ways. Even if they are not loud about their concern, others can feel the steady support that Virgo offers.

Down-to-Earth Wisdom

Because Virgos pay attention to what works in real life, they often have useful lessons to share. Over time, they gather experience from trying different approaches, reading, or observing how events unfold. This accumulation of knowledge can give them a sort of down-to-earth wisdom that friends value.

If someone is trying to decide how to approach a task, a Virgo might say, "Try these three simple steps," or "Here is what I've seen help others in the same spot." They might not claim to have all the answers, but they can suggest ideas backed by real examples. This practicality often helps others feel more confident about trying a solution.

In conflicts, a Virgo might also bring a balanced viewpoint. They can see where each person stands and may offer a calm middle ground. They strive to be fair, looking at the facts rather than siding blindly with one party. This balanced approach can guide groups toward better communication.

Steady Determination

While Virgos might not always show flashy excitement, they can have a quiet but firm determination. When they set their mind to something, they keep going until it is done. They might not talk about their goals non-stop, but they work toward them consistently.

This determination might show up in personal fitness, where a Virgo sets a target to run a certain distance and steadily increases their mileage. Or it could be seen in creative work, where they write or paint every day to reach a milestone. They prefer a slow-and-steady path, trusting that small daily efforts add up to big results in the end.

This strength helps them maintain their efforts even if they do not see quick outcomes. Others might quit early, but Virgo keeps at it because they trust the plan and the process. Over time, they often achieve steady growth and end up surprising those who did not notice their quiet progress.

Ability to Adapt Tools and Methods

Virgos often enjoy finding the right tools for a job. They might test various apps, gadgets, or procedures until they discover one that suits them. Once they do, they use it to make their tasks smoother. Their willingness to adapt tools to fit their needs is a special strength that can serve them well in many areas of life.

For example, if a Virgo needs to keep track of multiple tasks at school or work, they might try a few scheduling apps until they find one that is simple and effective. Then they customize how they sort tasks, color-code the categories, or set alarms. This can help them stay on top of responsibilities without feeling lost.

The same approach applies to household tasks. If a Virgo notices it takes too long to organize groceries each week, they might look for a better shopping list tool. Over time, they might refine this list to account for favorite foods, costs, or healthy choices. This practice of testing and refining is a quiet but powerful trait that often goes unnoticed.

Respect for Order and Cleanliness

While not all Virgos are neat, many do respect an orderly space. They may feel calmer when items are stored properly and surfaces are free of clutter. This does not mean they obsess over dirt or dust. Rather, they appreciate how a tidy area helps them think clearly.

This attitude can be a strength in places like labs, kitchens, or offices where organization really matters. By keeping everything labeled and in the right spot, they cut down on wasted time searching for things. This makes them efficient at tasks that need systematic planning or repeated checking.

Respect for order also extends to how Virgos handle rules or guidelines. They might read instructions carefully, then follow them exactly, knowing that doing so can prevent mishaps. This trust in structure can be beneficial in many roles, from professional settings to everyday household routines.

Quiet Encouragement

Virgos may not shout praises from the rooftops, but they can be encouraging in a gentle way. They might notice someone's improvement in a skill and give a small nod or a few kind words. Sometimes, this small gesture means a lot, because it feels sincere and not forced.

A Virgo might say, "I see how much better you've gotten at that," or "You really handled that situation well." These comments are often grounded in real examples, so they feel genuine. This kind of encouragement can spur people on to keep going, knowing that a Virgo is truly noticing their efforts.

Quiet encouragement can be especially nice for those who feel shy or uncertain. A Virgo's calm presence and real feedback help them believe in their ability to progress. While a loud cheer might be exciting, steady validation from someone who truly pays attention can be even more motivating in the long run.

Balanced Blend of Thinking and Doing

One final strength that stands out for Virgo is the way they blend thought and action. Some signs act first and think later; others plan a lot but struggle to take action. Virgo usually finds a balance. They think enough to avoid careless mistakes, but they also know that to get results, they must take steady steps.

This balance appears in everyday decisions. For instance, if they want to learn a new language, they study grammar but also practice speaking or writing right away. If they want to fix something in the house, they watch tutorials, gather the right tools, and then do the repair. This ability to switch between thinking mode and doing mode makes them very productive.

Such a skill is very handy in team settings. When people are stuck discussing an idea too long, a Virgo might say, "We have enough information to begin the first step." When others rush ahead without a plan, the Virgo might suggest stepping back to clarify the goal. In this way, Virgos help maintain a healthy pace that leads to real progress.

CHAPTER 6: COMMON CHALLENGES FOR VIRGO

While Virgo has many solid strengths, there are also challenges that can arise from the same qualities that make this sign special. Many Virgos may deal with worries about mistakes, or they might find it hard to relax because they aim for thoroughness in everything. Below, we explore the hurdles that Virgos commonly face. Each Virgo is different, so not every person with this sign will share all these issues. Still, these themes often appear and can affect how Virgo individuals feel about themselves and interact with the world.

Pressure to be Perfect

Virgos often pay close attention to details, which can be helpful. However, it can also lead to a strong desire for perfection. They might check their work multiple times, worried that a tiny mistake could ruin the entire effort. This worry can grow until it feels like a heavy load.

For example, a Virgo might finish a school project but then keep making minor changes until the last second. They might struggle to hand it in, thinking, "What if I missed something?" Even after turning it in, they might keep thinking about how it could have been improved. This self-pressure can rob them of the peace that comes from completing a task.

If perfectionism goes too far, it can become hard for a Virgo to start anything new. They might think, "I cannot begin until I have every single detail planned." This can slow their progress and cause them to miss out on experiences. Recognizing that perfection is not always possible, and that small mistakes can be learning points, may help them find balance.

Self-Criticism

Along with perfectionism, Virgos can be very hard on themselves. They might see a minor setback as a sign they are not good enough. This can hurt their confidence over time. Even when they achieve something, they might focus on the little flaws rather than celebrating the overall success.

For example, if a Virgo organizes an event and everything goes well except for one hiccup, they might dwell on that one issue. They may replay it in their mind, thinking how it could have been avoided, instead of feeling good about all the parts that went smoothly.

This self-criticism might also appear in small daily moments, like if they miss a word on a spelling quiz or forget to bring something to work. Instead of letting it go, they might feel upset with themselves for hours or days. Finding ways to be kinder to themselves, like listing what they did well, can help lessen this harsh inner voice.

Difficulty Delegating Tasks

Because Virgos like things done a certain way, they may find it challenging to let others take over tasks. They might worry that the other person will not handle details as carefully. This can lead to Virgos taking on more work than they can realistically manage.

In group efforts, a Virgo might keep control of most parts of the project. While this can ensure good quality, it can also cause them stress and exhaust them. They may lose sleep or skip breaks because they feel nobody else will do it correctly.

Learning to trust others and allow them to approach tasks in their own style can be a big step for Virgos. Delegation can free up time and energy. It also teaches them that different methods can still lead to good outcomes. If they can relax a bit about having full control, they might find more peace and less tension in shared activities.

Overthinking and Worry

Virgos might have a tendency to analyze situations from every angle. This can be a strength in solving problems, but it can also turn into overthinking. They might question every decision: "Is this the right job for me?" "Could I have said that better?" "What if this small choice leads to a major problem?"

This constant thinking can bring worry that is hard to shake off. A Virgo might lie awake at night, replaying events from the day or planning in detail for the next day. They might also worry about things that are out of their control, like world events or other people's reactions.

To handle this, it can help if Virgos set aside a short time to think about concerns and list possible solutions. Then, for the rest of the day, they practice letting go of those worries until their "worry time" comes again. This can help them avoid the cycle of endless thoughts that lead to stress.

Being Seen as Too Critical

While Virgos often want to help by offering tips or spotting issues, others might see this as criticism. If a Virgo points out small mistakes in a friend's plan, that friend might feel judged. The friend might not realize the Virgo is trying to prevent bigger problems later.

Over time, people might say, "You are too picky," or, "You only focus on what's wrong." This perception can hurt Virgos' relationships. Virgos may feel misunderstood because they see their comments as helpful, not hurtful.

Learning to deliver feedback gently can lessen these tensions. Instead of stating what is wrong right away, a Virgo might first note what is good, then carefully suggest an improvement. This approach can help others see the intent behind Virgo's advice without feeling attacked.

Stress from Clutter or Disorganization

Many Virgos prefer tidy spaces because it helps them think clearly. When they find themselves in a chaotic environment, it can make them feel uneasy or stressed. This might happen if they share a living space with someone who does not mind clutter.

In workplaces, too, disorganized settings might bother a Virgo. For instance, if files are scattered all over or if tasks are not clearly assigned, a Virgo might feel upset each time they try to work. They could attempt to organize everything themselves, but that can become a big burden.

Finding ways to communicate their need for order or setting small systems in place can help. For example, they could label storage boxes or create checklists that everyone can follow. This might reduce the sense that they must clean up or sort everything alone.

Reluctance to Show Emotions

Virgos can be careful about sharing their feelings. While they might be kind to others, they often guard their own emotions. They may not want to seem weak or out of control. This reluctance can lead them to keep worries or sadness hidden.

In relationships, this can cause confusion. Close friends or partners might feel that a Virgo is distant or not open. The Virgo might be having deep thoughts or worries but not saying them out loud. Over time, this can create misunderstandings, because the other person might think the Virgo is simply not interested.

Learning to share feelings in small steps can help. Virgos might start by telling a trusted friend or relative what is on their mind before it builds up too much. They do not have to reveal every thought, but small bits of openness can strengthen bonds and prevent isolation.

Setting Unrealistic Standards for Others

Virgos hold themselves to high standards, which can spill over to how they view the people around them. They might expect the same level of careful work from friends or teammates, without recognizing that others might have different approaches or strengths.

For instance, if a Virgo organizes a trip and expects others to follow the same precise plan, they might be upset if someone shows up late or forgets an item. The Virgo might think, "It was all in the schedule; why didn't they check?" Meanwhile, the other person might be more flexible about timing.

Finding a middle ground is essential. If Virgos can accept that everyone has unique ways of doing things, they may avoid disappointment and frustration. Allowing a bit more freedom in group settings can help them keep positive relationships.

Burnout from Constant Effort

Because Virgos often push themselves to be useful and to do tasks well, they might go a long time without rest. They might believe they have to keep going until everything is perfect. This can lead to burnout, where they feel exhausted, unmotivated, or even ill.

Burnout might show up as trouble sleeping, feeling cranky, or losing interest in things they usually enjoy. A Virgo might become annoyed by even small requests for help, because they feel they have no energy left to give. They might also find it harder to concentrate, making their usual detail-focused style more difficult.

Taking regular breaks and setting limits can protect against burnout. This might mean scheduling time off, even if it is just a calm evening without tasks. Doing something relaxing—like gentle stretching, reading a light book, or listening to calming music—can help them recharge. It is also helpful for Virgos to remind themselves that rest is not laziness but a necessary part of staying healthy.

Struggles with Spontaneity

Virgos often prefer to plan things in advance. If someone suddenly asks them to do something unexpected, they might feel uneasy. While some signs thrive on spur-of-the-moment events, Virgos might want to check their schedule, think about possible drawbacks, and then decide.

This can make them seem reluctant when friends want to go on a quick outing or try a new activity. Virgos might worry about what supplies they need, how long it will take, or whether it conflicts with other plans. Sometimes, they miss out on fun chances because they are not comfortable acting so quickly.

Balancing structure with a bit of openness can help. Virgos can learn to keep a small window of free time or to say yes to small surprises now and then. They might find that they actually enjoy the change of pace. Even if they feel a bit nervous at first, seeing that things can go well without a detailed plan might help them ease up over time.

Feeling Responsible for Everyone's Comfort

Virgos often like to help and can be very thoughtful. However, this can turn into feeling they must solve every problem or fix everyone's worries. They might take on the role of the caretaker and become stressed when issues arise that they cannot fix.

For instance, if friends are arguing, a Virgo might step in to mediate, even if it is not truly their role. Or if a family member is struggling with finances, a Virgo might feel they should offer their own money or resources, even if it puts them in a difficult position. They may blame themselves if the problem does not improve, thinking they did not do enough.

Realizing that some problems are not theirs to solve can bring relief. They can still show care and support, but they do not have to carry every burden alone. Understanding where their responsibility ends can help them keep healthy boundaries and protect their own well-being.

Getting Stuck in Small Details

While Virgos' focus on details is often a strength, it can become a challenge if they lose sight of the bigger picture. They might perfect one small part of a project but then run out of time for the rest. Or they might get hung up on a minor aspect that is less important in the long run.

For example, if they are decorating a room, they might spend hours picking the exact shade of paint while ignoring that the room also needs furniture or repairs. By the time they finally choose the paint, they might feel stressed about having no plan for the other parts of the room.

A helpful technique is to start with a general outline or a main goal. Once that is set, they can focus on small details. This "big picture first" method ensures they do not get so absorbed in one area that they neglect others.

Tendency to Bottleneck Group Projects

Virgos can be efficient workers, but if they handle too many vital steps alone, they might become a "bottleneck." That means progress stalls until they finish their part. Sometimes, this happens because they think, "I'm the only one who can do it right."

In a group project, this leads to slowdowns. Other members wait for the Virgo to complete their portion. Meanwhile, the Virgo is juggling multiple tasks, feeling overwhelmed. This can create tension, as others might grow impatient.

Stepping back and trusting teammates to manage certain tasks can free Virgos from this burden. Even if the result is not exactly the way the Virgo would have done it, it might still be acceptable or good. Learning to trust the competence of others can reduce stress and help the group move faster.

Trouble Accepting Praise

When friends or coworkers compliment them, Virgos might respond with something like, "It was nothing" or "I still could have done better." They tend to see flaws even in successful work. As a result, they rarely take time to feel proud of their accomplishments.

This can create a cycle where Virgos do great work but never feel satisfied. They move from one task to the next, always looking for what is lacking. Over time, this can lead to a sense of emptiness or feeling unappreciated, even though people do value them.

Accepting praise does not have to mean becoming boastful. Virgos can learn to say a simple "thank you" and allow themselves to feel pleased for a moment. It can be a step toward healthier self-esteem and motivation.

Running Low on Fun

Virgos may place strong emphasis on responsibilities. They might think, "I have so much to do, so little time for play." Although this can make them productive, it may also leave them missing out on relaxation and enjoyment. They can become so focused on tasks that they forget to include light-hearted activities.

Over an extended period, a lack of fun can dampen creativity and overall happiness. Sometimes, stepping away from tasks to do something purely enjoyable can refresh the mind. Even a short break can lead to new insights or solutions.

This is why it helps for Virgos to schedule small fun moments. It could be as simple as listening to favorite songs, taking a nature walk, or having a playful chat with a friend. By weaving in these moments, they maintain a better emotional balance and avoid feeling worn out by constant work.

Holding on to Regrets

Virgos might replay past mistakes in their minds, thinking about how they could have acted differently. This can lead them to feel regret for longer than necessary. Instead of using these moments as lessons and moving on, they might dwell on them, which can hurt their self-esteem.

For instance, if they said something unkind during an argument, they might keep replaying it, even after apologizing and being forgiven. They could worry that the other person is still upset, or they might keep blaming themselves.

It can help for Virgos to remind themselves that everyone makes mistakes. Apologies and learning from the error can be enough. Deciding to move forward, rather than staying stuck in regret, frees up mental energy for more positive pursuits.

Resisting New Methods

Because Virgos rely on what they know works, they might be hesitant to adopt new methods or technologies. They figure, "Why fix what is not broken?" This caution can be helpful if it prevents them from chasing every passing trend. But it can also cause them to miss helpful updates.

For instance, if there is a new software that makes a job easier, a Virgo might hesitate to learn it, thinking their old method is fine. Over time, they could fall behind in skills or miss ways to save effort.

Trying a small test of the new method can help. Virgos might keep their familiar process while giving the new one a short trial. If it proves effective, they can slowly shift. This step-by-step approach respects their need for careful analysis while also letting them benefit from progress.

Comparing Themselves to Others

Virgos might look around and notice how others do a task, then feel they must match or surpass that level. They might see someone else's neat schedule and think, "I must be just as organized," or notice a coworker's perfect presentation and think, "I should improve my speaking skills."

While comparing can sometimes motivate them, it can also create stress. They might forget that everyone has unique strengths and weaknesses. Feeling the need to compete at everything can lead to constant striving without real enjoyment.

A healthier approach is to set personal goals based on their own progress, rather than on what someone else does. This way, they can acknowledge their improvements over time and feel a sense of growth that does not rely on outdoing others.

Overcommitting

Virgos who want to be helpful might find themselves saying "yes" to too many requests. Because they do not like to let others down, they might accept tasks even if they are already busy. Over time, this can build up until they feel buried under obligations.

They might also hesitate to ask for help, believing they should handle everything on their own. This can lead to feeling trapped and exhausted. In serious cases, it might affect their health, such as developing stress-related symptoms.

Learning to set polite boundaries can solve this problem. They can let people know when their plate is full or suggest an alternative person who might help. They can also practice saying, "I'd love to help, but I need to check my other responsibilities first." This protects their energy and prevents burnout.

Fear of Letting Others Down

Finally, Virgos might carry a strong fear of disappointing people. They worry that if they do not perform perfectly, they will lose respect or affection. This fear can push them to try harder but can also make them anxious and hesitant.

They could be scared to take on a new project because they do not want to fail. Or they might avoid sharing an idea in a meeting, worried others might not like it. This fear can limit their potential and keep them from exploring new opportunities.

Learning to handle this fear involves understanding that most people appreciate honest effort, not flawless performance. If Virgos can open up about their concerns, they might find that friends and coworkers value them for who they are, not just for their success. Step by step, they can build the bravery to take on challenges without worrying so much about possible disappointment.

CHAPTER 7: VIRGO IN PERSONAL RELATIONSHIPS

Personal relationships can be a big part of life for many Virgos. Their caring nature and attention to small details often shape how they interact with partners, friends, and others they hold close. Even though each Virgo is unique, there are certain patterns that may emerge when we look at how Virgo qualities show up in personal bonds. Understanding these patterns can help both Virgos and the people around them find healthy ways to connect.

One of the first things people notice about Virgo in personal relationships is how helpful they can be. If a loved one has a concern, a Virgo might try to fix it with practical actions. For example, if a partner is tired after a difficult day, a Virgo may set up a cozy home environment or take care of chores. While other signs might offer an emotional pep talk, Virgos often show care by rolling up their sleeves and doing something that brings relief.

Virgos also value trust and dependability. In many cases, this means they show up on time and keep promises. A Virgo might make a special effort to be present at important events or to provide steady support during hard moments. This sense of reliability helps create a secure bond, because both partners know they can count on each other. However, it is also important for the Virgo's loved ones to understand that while Virgo is dependable, they may need room to recharge when they feel overwhelmed.

In romantic relationships, Virgos may move slowly at first. They often want to observe and gather facts about a potential partner before committing. Some might even create a mental list of what they want in a relationship—values, habits, or life goals—though they may not say it out loud. This careful approach can make them seem cautious. Others might mistake it for a lack of warmth. In truth, Virgos can be very warm once they decide to invest in the bond.

Because of their detail-focused thinking, Virgos may notice small habits or subtle changes in a partner's behavior. If a partner is upset, Virgos might pick up on it even if that person does not speak about it. This can be comforting, because it feels like someone is truly paying attention. However, it can also cause confusion if the partner does not want to discuss those feelings yet. Virgos might push for a practical way to address the sadness, while the partner might not be ready to talk. Striking a balance is key.

Communication is another interesting area for Virgos in relationships. Many Virgos like to talk about real-world concerns, such as scheduling, budgeting, or solving problems. They might not be as quick to speak about dreams or unproven ideas. For instance, if someone proposes a big plan without details, a Virgo could respond by asking, "How will we handle the cost?" or "Is there a good timeline?" This focus on facts can keep a partnership grounded, but it also helps if the Virgo occasionally leaves room for fun ideas without picking them apart right away.

When it comes to romantic gestures, Virgos may prefer everyday acts of kindness over grand displays. They might fix a leaky tap, prepare a meal, or organize a partner's workspace as a way to show affection. Some partners might misunderstand this, wishing for more obvious romance. If that happens, it helps to remember that Virgo often expresses care by doing things. A Virgo may not say "I love you" repeatedly, but they often show it through consistent attention and service.

On the other hand, Virgos might struggle if their partner is very disorganized. Because Virgo thrives in calm and neat spaces, a messy living area can feel stressful. Discussions about tidiness might pop up, and the Virgo could seem controlling when they point out the need for cleaning. However, from Virgo's perspective, order is linked to peace of mind. Open communication about personal preferences can prevent conflicts, helping each person see why certain things matter so much.

Another factor in Virgo relationships is the sign's link to personal growth. Many Virgos care about improving day-to-day life. They might encourage a partner to adopt healthier routines or to learn new skills. While this can be inspiring, it may also feel like pressure if done too forcefully. A partner could think, "Why is Virgo pointing out all the ways I can improve?" To avoid this, Virgos can frame their suggestions as gentle options rather than must-do tasks.

When problems arise, Virgos may try to solve them with a methodical approach. They might talk it through, suggesting steps or listing pros and cons. This can help couples tackle real-world problems, like finances or scheduling conflicts. Yet, if the issue is more emotional, the Virgo approach might feel too logical to a partner who wants comfort or empathy. In that case, it can help Virgos to simply listen first, offering a caring presence instead of solutions.

In more casual dating, Virgos might be particular about who they choose to see. They do not always date many people at once, because they prefer quality over quantity. They could be turned off if someone's behavior seems too careless. However, if they meet someone who shows both kindness and consistency, Virgo's interest may grow. Their attention to detail means they will likely remember small facts about their date—favorite meals, favorite books, or a problem mentioned in passing. This can be endearing, as it proves the Virgo is truly paying attention.

Arguments or disagreements can be challenging. Virgos might respond by calmly pointing out the facts of the situation. They might say, "You said this on Tuesday, which doesn't match what you're saying now." This method can feel like they are keeping score. Partners who do not think in a detail-focused way may feel cornered. One approach to preventing this is for Virgos to give more space for feelings, rather than sticking solely to facts. If they learn to acknowledge emotions before moving into analysis, discussions can be more balanced.

Virgos can form strong bonds with those who appreciate their quiet support. In friendships, Virgo's personal relationships often revolve around being reliable. If a friend needs help moving or organizing, the Virgo friend may show up right away with a plan. In romantic situations, the same dependability can come across as devotion. Over time, this creates trust. However, Virgos should also keep an eye on whether they are giving too much without receiving enough care in return. Sometimes, Virgos pour effort into people who do not appreciate them.

For Virgo parents or family members, the desire to look after loved ones might be very strong. They can be the ones who plan family dinners, keep track of birthdays, or ensure that each person gets the support they need. The family might rely on the Virgo relative for these important tasks. Though this can be rewarding, it can also pile up responsibilities. Virgos might want to share the workload to avoid feeling overwhelmed, even if they believe others might not do the tasks as "perfectly."

In personal relationships, Virgos may also deal with their own self-criticism. If they feel they are not meeting their partner's expectations, they can become anxious. They might blame themselves for minor arguments or small mistakes. A loving partner can help by reminding Virgo that imperfection is normal. Learning to forgive themselves allows Virgo to show up more calmly in the relationship, without trying to manage every detail perfectly.

Sometimes, Virgos pick partners or friends who match their Earthy nature, like Taurus or Capricorn. These Earth signs share a preference for stability and a practical approach to life. Still, Virgos can also do well with signs that balance their traits, like Water signs that bring emotional depth, or Fire signs that bring enthusiasm. However, no zodiac match is guaranteed. Communication, mutual respect, and empathy matter more than just sign compatibility.

One area where Virgos might shine is planning shared activities. They might organize day trips or quiet weekends at home, making sure all details are covered. This can remove stress for the partner, who only has to show up and enjoy. Yet, to avoid making it all about chores and lists, Virgos could remember to include some unplanned time for relaxation. This flexible space might lead to fun surprises and a closer emotional bond.

Affection in Virgo relationships might not be loud, but it can be steady. A Virgo partner might softly check on a loved one's well-being or share simple words of support at the end of the day. These small moments matter. They show that Virgo is always watching out for changes in mood, trying to protect the health of the bond. Over time, these tiny gestures can bring a sense of security that a more dramatic sign might not offer.

Of course, there can be conflicts if a Virgo seems too controlling. For instance, if a partner has a different cleaning style, a Virgo may step in and insist on their methods. Over time, the partner may feel like they are always being directed. To keep peace, Virgos should remember that everyone has unique ways of doing things. Some tasks might be worth letting go or splitting up rather than insisting on a single "correct" way.

When it comes to resolving tension, Virgos might benefit from practicing patience with emotions. If a partner is upset, it helps for Virgo to listen without rushing to fix the problem. They can ask questions like, "How are you feeling?" or "What do you think might help you right now?" Instead of diving into problem-solving, they can give a bit of gentle attention first. After the emotional side is addressed, they can offer solutions if the partner wants them.

In more mature Virgo relationships, there is often a pattern of continuous improvement. The couple might refine daily routines or set up better communication methods over time. This can keep the partnership running smoothly. However, it's important that not every talk turns into a "How can we improve this?" discussion. Partners also need simple closeness and fun, free from the urge to perfect everything.

Because Virgos take relationships seriously, they might be less likely to leap from one romance to another. When they do settle into a bond, they usually put in the effort to make it strong. The downside is that if the relationship becomes unhealthy or the partner is disrespectful, Virgo might stick around too long, hoping they can fix it. They should remember that not all problems can be solved by more effort. Sometimes, leaving a harmful situation is healthier than staying.

Another topic that can arise is the Virgo's tendency to worry. This might lead them to double-check a partner's words or actions, fearing something hidden. If they see small signs that could indicate trouble, they may overanalyze them. This can put strain on both sides. In such cases, open communication can help. If the partner reassures Virgo calmly and consistently, it may ease those worries. Virgos should also try to trust the relationship when things are going well, rather than always looking for issues.

Virgos often value honest talk. They can become upset if they feel a partner is not telling the truth or hiding key facts. Some Virgos might even ask direct questions to be sure they understand everything. This honesty can build a deep connection, but it must be balanced with kindness. A partner might feel interrogated if Virgo asks too many detailed questions at once. Learning to phrase questions softly and accept answers without too much doubt can be key to smooth interaction.

Over time, a stable Virgo relationship can bring comfort, support, and steady growth. Virgos tend to be devoted, practical, and caring. They want to see their loved ones thrive. If they can learn to relax some of their standards and recognize that every person has quirks, they become more accepting partners. Meanwhile, their steady presence often gives the other person a feeling of being truly valued. This balance of practical help and warm reliability is what many cherish about Virgos in personal relationships.

In summary, Virgos approach personal bonds with a serious mind and a big heart. They aim to care for their partners or close friends in tangible ways, offering real assistance and thoughtful gestures. They also place great importance on reliability, honesty, and steady communication. Tension can arise when they attempt to manage all details or slip into excessive self-criticism. However, with open dialogue and an understanding approach, Virgos can form personal relationships that last, providing a stable home base for both themselves and their loved ones.

CHAPTER 8: EMOTIONAL LIFE OF A VIRGO

Though Virgos are often known for their practical and organized nature, they also have emotional sides that may not be clear to everyone. Underneath their calm surface, many Virgos experience a range of feelings, from kindness to worry. Understanding Virgo's emotional world can help you see that they are not just detail-focused planners. They also care deeply about how they and others feel.

A common assumption is that Virgos are not very emotional because they tend to communicate in calm, logical ways. In reality, Virgos can be sensitive. They simply prefer to manage their emotions with logic. For example, if something upsets them, they might first think about how to solve it or how to organize their feelings into clear thoughts. This does not mean they lack strong emotions. It just means their style of handling them might appear different from, say, a Water sign.

One aspect of Virgo's emotional life is their tendency toward worry. Because they notice details and think things through in depth, they can anticipate possible problems. This can keep them from acting impulsively, but it can also lead to anxiety if they imagine every negative outcome. For instance, a Virgo might worry about a simple medical test, thinking about all the rare problems that could arise. To ease this, they may try reading facts or data, hoping to calm themselves by seeing that the chance of serious trouble is low.

Virgos can also feel frustrated when things around them seem chaotic. Their emotional well-being often depends on having at least some control over their environment. If a family member is very messy, a Virgo might feel off-balance until the space is tidied up. Likewise, if schedules and plans keep changing, they might experience stress. These changes can shake the sense of calm that Virgos build by having clear routines.

When Virgos do feel strong emotions, they might keep them hidden. They may prefer to process them in private rather than talk openly. This can lead to friends or loved ones thinking the Virgo is not bothered at all. In truth, the Virgo might be quietly dealing with feelings, journaling about them, or going for a walk to clear their head. Learning to share some of these emotions can help them feel closer to others, especially if the people around them are patient and understanding.

Despite their reserved nature, Virgos can be very empathetic. They often pick up on small cues that reveal how others are doing emotionally. If a friend looks sad but tries to hide it, the Virgo might notice the change in tone or body language. This awareness can make them compassionate listeners. However, they may respond by offering practical advice instead of purely emotional support. While that advice might be helpful, some people just want a hug or a few kind words instead.

An interesting point about Virgo's emotional life is how they react to praise or compliments. On one hand, they want to do a good job and like knowing people see their efforts. On the other hand, they may feel uncomfortable receiving praise. They might downplay their achievements or point out flaws in what they did. This can puzzle others who want to celebrate their efforts. In reality, the Virgo might feel shy about being in the spotlight. They may also see every small mistake, overshadowing the bigger success.

Virgos can also struggle with guilt if they think they have let someone down. Because they hold themselves to high standards, failing a promise or making a slip in a relationship can weigh heavily on them. They might replay the situation over and over, wondering how they could have behaved differently. Sometimes, this guilt lingers even after the other person has forgiven them. Learning to forgive themselves is an important step in balancing their emotions.

In group settings, Virgo's emotional side can lean toward caution. They might not be the first to speak up or share personal stories. Instead, they observe, waiting to see if the space is safe for vulnerability. Over time, if they feel comfortable, they may open up more. However, they might still prefer one-on-one talks over large gatherings, because smaller groups often allow for deeper and calmer connections.

When Virgos do share their feelings, they usually do it in a careful, structured way. They might say, "I felt upset when this event happened because it reminded me of a similar moment in the past." Others might share emotions in a big wave, but Virgos tend to explain them with reasons and background. This can be good for solving emotional conflicts, but it can also feel a bit reserved. Some might wish the Virgo would express raw feelings without analysis. Finding a middle ground—where Virgo can still organize thoughts but also let feelings flow—can help them relate more closely to people who need direct emotional expressions.

Another key point is how Virgos handle disappointment. If something goes wrong, they may look inward, wondering if they could have prevented it. While self-reflection is helpful, it can turn into self-blame if taken too far. For instance, if a friend decides to move away, a Virgo might wonder if they could have done something to make that friend stay. Recognizing that some events are not under their control helps Virgos avoid feeling burdened with unfair responsibility.

Virgos may also have a strong internal critic. This can influence their emotions by making them question if they have done enough or done things correctly. If they try a new hobby and it doesn't go well at first, they might quickly feel discouraged. Emotions like shame or frustration can arise, even if it is just part of the normal learning process. Practicing self-compassion—saying, "It is normal to make mistakes when trying something new"—can help.

Interestingly, Virgos often find peace in routines. A regular schedule, a familiar morning ritual, or a weekly cleanup can soothe them. This sense of order can be healing because it reduces the unknown. When life feels too random, their emotional state might become uneasy. If they sense chaos growing, they might respond by focusing even more on small tasks. In moderation, this coping method helps them stay grounded.

At times, Virgos might be too private about strong emotions like sadness or anger. They might fear that showing anger will hurt others' feelings or damage their own image as a composed person. However, bottling up such feelings can lead to resentment or stress in the long run. Finding a safe way to let out these emotions—talking to a trusted friend, writing in a journal, or doing a calming activity—can free them from emotional buildup.

In romantic relationships, a Virgo's emotional world can be both sweet and complex. They might deeply care about their partner's feelings, checking in quietly to see if everything is okay. If they sense tension, they may try to fix it. Yet, they might not always share their own emotional concerns unless asked. A partner who learns to notice subtle signs—a shift in mood, a hint of restlessness—can help the Virgo open up. Over time, this mutual understanding can make for a stable, nurturing bond.

When Virgos are happy, their emotions might show in simple acts. They might hum while doing chores or plan a treat for themselves, like a favorite snack. Although they might not jump and shout with glee, their contentment shows in a calm glow. People close to them can sense this peaceful mood. During these times, Virgos might also do small generous acts for others, reflecting their content inner state.

Sadness can appear when Virgos feel they are failing to meet their own standards or when they sense chaos they cannot control. In these moments, they might withdraw, spending extra time alone. They could become quieter and less energetic, focusing on tasks as a distraction. Loved ones who notice can encourage them to talk it out. While Virgo might not open up right away, gentle patience can help them feel safe enough to share what is on their mind.

Stress often appears for Virgos when they juggle too many tasks or worry about letting people down. Because they pride themselves on being dependable, they might push themselves until they are exhausted. Their emotions under stress can include anxiety, irritability, or feeling that things are spinning out of control. When they reach this point, taking breaks, getting fresh air, or engaging in a calming routine can help restore balance. They also benefit from learning that saying "no" to extra requests is sometimes necessary.

Despite these challenges, Virgo's emotional side can also be quite loving. Virgos often think deeply about the well-being of the people they care about. If a friend or partner is in trouble, they might worry more than the person going through the issue. Their empathy can inspire them to research solutions, bring comfort items, or check in consistently until the problem eases. People sometimes fail to notice this depth because Virgos do not always talk about it openly. But under their practical shell, there is a caring heart.

In social circles, Virgo's emotional stance can be that of the calm helper. They might be the one who quietly pulls someone aside to ask if they are okay during a hectic party or event. While they may not be the life of the party, they can be a steady presence who offers calm conversation or a listening ear. This low-key approach draws people who appreciate sincerity over flashiness.

When Virgos face bigger life changes, their emotions can become extra complex. For example, moving to a new city, switching jobs, or starting a major relationship can spark both excitement and nervousness. They might feel worried about all the unknowns but also hopeful about the fresh start. To cope, they often plan carefully, aiming to reduce uncertainty. This approach is how they balance the swirl of new feelings with their logical side.

As they grow older, many Virgos learn to handle their emotions with more acceptance. They might realize that not every worry deserves deep thought, and that mistakes or changes are part of life. Some develop routines like short meditation, gentle stretches, or calming crafts to quiet the mind. Others discover that simply talking with a close friend can release the tension that builds when they keep feelings under wraps.

Virgos who work on self-awareness may become skilled at calming both their own emotions and those of others. They can guide friends or family members through stressful times by suggesting helpful steps. Their calm nature and careful listening can create a safe space for others to unload worries. This is one reason people often describe Virgos as "grounding" friends who help keep everything under control.

On the flip side, if Virgos do not address their emotional side, they can feel a sense of emptiness or constant worry. They might try to fill this gap by focusing even more on tasks or routines. However, ignoring emotional needs rarely solves the underlying issues. A healthy approach might be to identify a few trusted people they can confide in. Even brief, honest conversations about stress or sadness can ease the load.

Ultimately, the emotional life of a Virgo is a subtle blend of careful thought, empathy, worry, and a wish for stability. They care deeply about doing things right and looking after the people around them. Though they may seem reserved, they experience an active inner world filled with hopes, concerns, and compassion. When they learn to manage their self-criticism and share feelings in balanced ways, they can find greater peace. They also become able to give and receive love more freely.

For anyone who cares about a Virgo, recognizing these quieter feelings can go a long way. Encouraging them to speak up, gently reminding them that they do not have to fix everything, and praising their efforts in a genuine way can build their sense of security. In return, Virgos offer a grounded presence that keeps relationships honest and real. Their combination of emotional insight and practical thinking can bring calm in a world that often feels chaotic.

All in all, Virgos are much more than neat or logical people. Beneath their even-tempered exterior lies a heart that feels deeply, worries honestly, and loves steadfastly. They just have a special method for filtering these emotions through the lens of logic and order. By acknowledging the role of feelings in their lives and giving themselves permission to share those feelings, Virgos can create a rich emotional environment—one that benefits both them and the people who value their gentle guidance.

CHAPTER 9: VIRGO IN WORK AND CAREER

Introduction to Virgo's Work Style

Virgos often take their responsibilities seriously. In many workplaces, they can be the people who pay attention to the finer points and keep tasks in order. While some might think of Virgos only as perfectionists, there is much more depth to how they act in a professional setting. In this chapter, we will look at their work habits, how they manage tasks, and what sorts of jobs might be a good match for them. We will also discuss how Virgos interact with bosses, coworkers, and any challenges they could face in a career.

Planning and Organization

A big trait of Virgo is their strong sense of organization. This can show in how they handle daily tasks, keep track of files, or plan schedules. They might enjoy putting things in labeled folders or creating checklists to ensure that all work steps are covered. This behavior helps them stay calm and confident in high-pressure situations. While many people might see planning as dull, Virgos often see it as a way to maintain order. A well-structured plan can reduce errors, which is a main concern for those who dislike messy work.

Attention to Detail

When it comes to noticing the little things, Virgo is often second to none. If a project has small mistakes, a Virgo is likely to spot them quickly. For example, they might find spelling errors in a report that everyone else has passed over. They might notice if the numbers in a spreadsheet are off by just a small amount. This detail-focused outlook can be an advantage in fields where precision matters, like editing, bookkeeping, research, or data management. Coworkers might learn to rely on Virgo to catch errors and improve the quality of the final product.

Problem-Solving Strengths

Virgos tend to be logical thinkers who can analyze problems in an orderly way. Instead of feeling stuck or frustrated when a challenge appears, they often break it down into steps they can tackle one by one. This calm approach makes them good at troubleshooting tech issues, organizing complex events, or guiding a group through a tricky project. By focusing on each element of a problem, they reduce the sense of being overwhelmed. Others might admire how Virgos keep a level head instead of jumping to fast but unreliable answers.

Reliable Work Ethic

Being reliable is another strong point for Virgo in the workplace. Many Virgos show up on time, turn in projects by the deadline, and do their best to follow company rules. They may not always shine in the spotlight, but they are often the backbone that holds teams together. This dependable style can earn them a reputation for being someone who can be trusted. Bosses may quickly see that a Virgo handles tasks without constant reminders, and coworkers might feel confident partnering with them on important assignments.

Possible Career Paths

There are many fields where Virgo traits can shine. Some Virgos do well in areas involving research, data, or analysis. Others find that their attention to detail is helpful in the healthcare sector, where careful work can be crucial for a patient's care. Yet others might do well in creative roles that require precise editing, design, or planning, like being a writer, graphic artist, or crafts maker who values fine detail. Because Virgos can be service-minded, they might also excel in roles where they help people, such as counseling, teaching, or social work—especially if they learn to handle their own perfectionism.

Team Dynamics

When working on group projects, Virgos can be the ones who lay out a clear path. They might outline who handles which tasks, set realistic deadlines, and monitor progress to make sure nobody falls behind. This can be very useful in preventing confusion. However, Virgos should be mindful not to take over or appear too controlling. If they are always pointing out others' flaws or pushing for things to be done "the correct way," tension can arise. The best approach is to offer guidance without ignoring the team's ideas.

Virgos as Leaders

Even though some Virgos prefer working behind the scenes, they can become good leaders if they feel confident in their role. Their logical thinking helps them give clear directions, and they usually keep track of important details so the team does not miss anything. If they are in a leadership position, Virgos should remember that not all employees have the same knack for being organized. Allowing a bit of freedom and listening to each worker's style can help them earn respect and loyalty from their team members.

Challenges with Delegation

One ongoing struggle for Virgos is learning to delegate tasks. They often fear that if someone else handles the job, it might not be done to the highest standard. As a result, they might end up doing more work than is reasonable, risking burnout. In a busy career, this can lead to stress, long work hours, and feeling overwhelmed. However, letting others help can actually improve results, especially if coworkers bring their own talents or fresh ideas. Trusting a colleague's abilities can lighten Virgo's load and teach them about teamwork.

Handling Workplace Criticism

Because Virgos often hold high standards, they might feel hurt if someone criticizes their work. They might take it personally, worrying that they have failed. At the same time, they can be quick to point out issues they see in others' work, which might cause friction. It can help Virgos to find a balanced way of giving and receiving feedback. Before sharing critiques, they can note what is going well. When receiving feedback, they can remember that not all comments are a personal attack. Sometimes, it is simply a chance to improve.

Perfectionism and Time Management

Virgos' perfectionist side can slow them down if they are not careful. While it is great that they want tasks done well, spending hours on minor details can stall progress. Over time, they might realize that not every single part has to be perfect to meet the project's goals. Good time management can help. They can learn to prioritize the core tasks while letting some minor points remain "good enough." Recognizing that it is often better to complete an assignment well rather than keep perfecting it until it is late can ease pressure.

Workplace Anxiety and Stress

Virgos might experience anxiety when projects have unclear guidelines or when their plans change at the last minute. They prefer knowing what to expect, and quick changes can feel jarring.

In some jobs, this is simply part of the environment. To manage stress, Virgos can keep flexible backup plans. For instance, if a plan shifts, they can look for the next best option and adapt. Simple methods like short breaks, organized notes, or even talking to a supportive coworker can help them stay balanced instead of letting worry take over.

Virgos and Ethics

A Virgo's sense of right and wrong can be strong. They often prefer workplaces that match their personal ethics. If a company's values do not line up with a Virgo's moral beliefs, they may feel uneasy. When faced with unethical behavior, they might have trouble staying quiet, because they usually want fairness. This can be good for keeping standards high, but it could also cause conflicts if the company culture is not open to change. Still, many Virgos feel better in a job if they know it does not clash with their sense of honesty.

Communication Style at Work

Virgos typically communicate in a clear, factual way. They might use short emails or instructions, going straight to the point. This can be a strength, because it reduces confusion. Still, some coworkers might see this as cold or too direct. Learning how to include a friendly greeting or a short, positive note can help. Finding balance between being precise and being approachable can make Virgos more effective communicators. They might also practice pausing to see if the other person has questions, rather than assuming all details are already clear.

Cooperation with Different Personalities

Every workplace has a mix of personalities. Since Virgos are structured, they might clash with those who prefer spontaneity. For example, a coworker might show up with a new idea at the last minute, forcing a Virgo to adjust. On the flip side, Virgos might struggle with teammates who are messy or who do not meet deadlines. Learning to compromise can help everyone. Virgos can explain why organization is needed, while also accepting that not everyone thinks the same way. They may find that some variety in methods can lead to fresh perspectives.

Staying Motivated and Focused

One thing that keeps Virgos motivated is a sense of purpose. If their work feels useful, they are more likely to stay engaged. They might enjoy roles where they see visible results, such as completing a project that makes a customer happy or finishing a report that helps the company move forward. Small achievements along the way can keep them going. Setting specific goals—like finishing an important piece of work by noon—can give them short targets to hit, which is satisfying for someone who loves checking items off a list.

Boundaries and Work-Life Balance

Because they want to do tasks properly, Virgos can sometimes let work consume them. They might answer emails after hours or keep thinking about tasks during personal time. This can lead to exhaustion if they do not set boundaries. It is important for Virgos to learn that rest allows them to come back stronger the next day. Practical steps include turning off work notifications at a certain time or scheduling hobbies that help them unwind. By protecting their free time, Virgos can remain more effective during work hours.

Career Growth and Learning

Many Virgos love to learn new skills, and they might improve their knowledge on their own. They may watch tutorials, read articles, or take notes from experts to get better at their job. Over time, this can make them highly skilled, and they can become a key resource in their field. Employers often value someone who strives for constant improvement. However, Virgos should also be careful not to put too much pressure on themselves. Sometimes, it is okay to acknowledge that they have enough skill for the moment and do not need to master everything overnight.

Entrepreneurship and Virgo

Some Virgos decide to start their own businesses. Their detail-focused mindset can be a plus in tasks like budgeting, tracking expenses, and planning. They might excel at making sure they handle orders promptly or maintain good records. However, being a boss to oneself can also be tricky. A Virgo entrepreneur may find it hard to let anyone else help, or they might worry about every small risk. A balanced approach—where they slowly bring in helpers or advisors—can keep them from being overwhelmed and allow the business to grow steadily.

Handling Rapid Change

In fast-changing fields—like technology or advertising—Virgos can feel stressed by quick shifts in direction. One day, a client wants one thing; the next day, they want the opposite. While a certain amount of planning is good, some environments require a more flexible mindset. If Virgo works in such a setting, they may need to develop routines that help them adapt smoothly. For instance, they can keep updated notes on any changes, so they do not lose track. They can also practice stepping back to look at the overall picture rather than sweating each twist.

Dealing with Workplace Conflict

When disagreements arise, Virgos might rely on logic to solve them. They could lay out the pros and cons, hoping everyone sees the sensible option. But not all conflicts are purely logical; feelings might be involved. If a coworker is upset for personal reasons, simply showing them a list of facts might not help. Virgos who learn to validate emotions as well as reason can become excellent peacemakers. They can step in with a calm presence and show empathy while also guiding the discussion toward solutions that work for everyone.

Virgo's Approach to Deadlines

Meeting deadlines is often a Virgo's strong point, provided they were given clear instructions from the start. If the deadline is too soon, they might stress out. Some Virgos handle this by making micro-deadlines. For example, if a report is due in a week, they decide to finish the draft in three days, then edit it in the next two, leaving time for final checks. This step-by-step plan helps them avoid last-minute rush. Employers or clients often appreciate this reliability, as it means fewer surprises.

Team Mentoring

A Virgo who grows skilled in their field can be a good mentor for junior coworkers. They can pass along tips on how to organize tasks or maintain accuracy. They might show them better ways to structure a presentation or keep track of daily goals. The main challenge is not overwhelming the newcomer with too many details at once. By giving information in small steps, a Virgo can help others learn without feeling lost. This mentoring style can improve the overall quality of work in the team or department.

Satisfaction in Work

Ultimately, Virgos feel happier at work when they can see that their careful methods lead to positive outcomes. This might be a well-run office, a design project that looks polished, or a service that truly helps clients. They often do not need flashy praise, but they appreciate it when people notice the solid effort they put in. Over time, a Virgo who is allowed to use their organizational strengths will likely thrive. They want to feel that their role makes a difference, whether it is through perfect paperwork or a flawless final product.

Summary: Virgo's Career Outlook

To sum up, Virgos bring a set of strong traits to the workplace: keen attention to detail, a reliable work ethic, and practical problem-solving skills. Their sense of order can help them shine in careers that value thoroughness. Still, they may face issues like perfectionism, stress from messy environments, or difficulty letting others pitch in. By learning to balance their high standards with flexibility, Virgos can avoid burnout and keep growing in their roles. When they find a job that allows them to be precise and helpful, they often make a lasting impact and form a stable, fulfilling career path.

Final Thoughts on Virgo's Work and Career

Virgos' approach to their jobs is driven by an urge to do things correctly. They want to create structures that protect against errors and keep everything flowing. While this can sometimes seem strict, it often leads to results that are consistent and well-crafted. If Virgos can remember to stay open to new methods and let others share tasks, they can make a real difference in any job they pick. By allowing themselves moments of rest and acknowledging that not everything must be perfect, they will likely find a satisfying career that matches their natural skills.

CHAPTER 10: VIRGO AT HOME AND DAILY LIFE

Introduction to Virgo's Home Environment

At home, Virgo often seeks a place that feels calm and organized. They might see their living space as a reflection of their inner sense of order. Though each Virgo's style is unique, there are common themes in how they manage their household, daily tasks, and personal routines. We will look at how they handle chores, manage their time, and build comforting rituals that keep them balanced.

Preference for Tidiness

While not every Virgo is a spotless cleaner, many do appreciate neat surroundings. It might bother them to have clutter piling up. They could be the type to fold laundry right away, keep dishes washed, or put items back in their proper spots. This sense of tidiness is not only about appearances; it also helps them feel that life is under control. When their environment is orderly, Virgos may experience less stress and more mental clarity.

Practical Home Routines

Daily routines can be very important to a Virgo. Having a fixed time for waking up, eating meals, or handling chores can help them feel grounded. They might plan out their week on a calendar, noting the best times for tasks like grocery shopping or cleaning. This practical approach helps them avoid last-minute hassles. For instance, if they need groceries, they might make a list in advance, double-check what is already at home, and only then head out. Such planning can save time and reduce waste.

Kitchen Habits and Meal Preparation

In the kitchen, Virgos might be quite methodical. They could measure ingredients precisely and arrange their pantry so that it is easy to see what needs restocking. Some might enjoy cooking because it blends creativity with an organized process. A Virgo cook might try new recipes in a structured way, following each step carefully and making small notes to refine the dish next time. This is not about being fancy, but rather about getting consistent results. Their attention to detail often pays off when it comes to flavor and presentation.

Decorating and Arrangement

When choosing how to decorate their home, many Virgos prefer a clean, simple look over a very flashy style. They might favor neutral colors or subtle patterns that create a peaceful mood. If they display items, those pieces often have a practical purpose or sentimental meaning. Virgo might keep a cozy reading nook or a well-ordered desk with everything in its place. They may also enjoy having some plants if they can look after them consistently. The key is finding a balance between comfort and order, so their space feels both welcoming and efficient.

Managing Household Tasks

Virgos often excel at setting up schedules for household chores. They might divide tasks by day—for example, vacuuming on one day, laundry on another, and so forth. By spreading out chores, they avoid feeling overwhelmed. If they live with others, they might try to assign jobs so everyone helps. However, a Virgo can become frustrated if housemates do not do their share or do not do it to the standard the Virgo expects. Learning to be flexible and meeting others halfway can prevent conflicts and keep a pleasant home atmosphere.

Balancing Work and Personal Life at Home

In the age of remote work, many Virgos find that the lines between job tasks and home life can blur. Because they like being efficient, they may slip into the habit of checking work messages at odd hours. To maintain balance, Virgos can set clear boundaries. For instance, they might create a small workspace separate from the rest of the living area, so they can "leave" work once the day ends. Simple boundaries like not answering emails after a certain hour can protect their personal time.

Relaxation and Hobbies

Though Virgos can be serious at times, they still benefit from relaxing hobbies. Some may enjoy puzzle games, crafting, or reading as ways to calm a busy mind. Activities that offer both structure and creativity can be especially appealing. For example, a Virgo might like knitting because it follows a pattern while still allowing for personal touches in color or design. Others might prefer writing down thoughts in a journal, savoring the routine of setting aside a few minutes each day to reflect.

Hosting Guests and Social Gatherings

When Virgos invite friends over, they often plan carefully. They might clean up the house more than usual, arrange seating so it is practical, or ensure that refreshments are ready beforehand. They want their guests to feel comfortable and may pay attention to small details—like having enough clean plates or checking if anyone has dietary preferences. However, hosting can also be stressful if they strive for perfection. It can help them relax if they remind themselves that people are there to enjoy good company, not to judge the smallest flaws.

Handling Clutter Buildup

Over time, any home can gather clutter, and Virgos are not immune to this. The difference is that they might be more bothered by it than some other signs. If papers, clothes, or unused items start piling up, a Virgo could feel mentally heavy. Periodic decluttering can restore a sense of peace. Some Virgos use a simple rule: if something has not been used in a year, consider donating or recycling it. This keeps their living space from turning into a storage place for old or unwanted things.

Virgo's Approach to Personal Health at Home

Health often matters to Virgos, so they might incorporate routines to stay well. They could set up an exercise spot or keep healthy foods ready in the fridge. Some might track their meals or follow certain eating guidelines if they feel it boosts their energy. While this can be a positive habit, Virgos should guard against being too rigid. A balanced approach—where they allow themselves occasional treats or rest days—can keep them from burning out on strict rules.

Setting Up a Calm Atmosphere

Virgos often crave a calm living area that helps them decompress after a busy day. They might keep noise levels low, play gentle music, or light softly scented candles. Their goal is usually to create an environment that supports focus and relaxation. Because they notice small disturbances easily, they may avoid having the TV on loudly or living in a space with too many bright, clashing colors. Each choice points toward harmony and mental peace.

Daily Planning Tools

One of Virgo's favorite tools might be a planner or a digital app for tasks. They can schedule important activities like bill payments, doctor appointments, or errands. This helps them avoid the anxiety of forgetting deadlines. Checking off completed items can give them a sense of success, even for small tasks. If they live with family or roommates, they might share a calendar so everyone knows the plan. This can reduce last-minute scrambles over who is doing what and when.

Personal Projects and DIY

Some Virgos like to handle small home improvements or repairs themselves. They might watch tutorials or read step-by-step guides on how to fix a dripping faucet or paint a room neatly. This approach appeals to their practical nature and can save money. However, they need to watch out for perfectionist tendencies that lead them to spend too long on a simple task. If a project becomes too big or complex, getting expert help can prevent frustration.

Energy and Mood in the Home

Because Virgos can be sensitive to messy energies, they might rearrange furniture or clean surfaces if they sense something feels "off." This is not just about the look of the space; it is about the mood they pick up when they walk into a room. Even small actions—like opening windows for fresh air or adding plants—can make them feel better. Some Virgos also like to keep their rooms bright and tidy because it lifts their spirits, helping them avoid negative emotions that come from chaos.

Pet Care

If a Virgo chooses to have pets, they often take good care of them. They might follow a clear feeding schedule or research the best kind of food. They usually keep the pet's area clean, checking that everything is fresh and in order. While it can be extra work, many Virgos do not mind because they see the pet's well-being as an important duty. This sense of structure can be positive for pets, who thrive on routine and consistent attention.

Financial Organization at Home

Handling personal finances is another area where Virgo's careful mindset helps. They might keep receipts filed, plan a budget, and monitor expenses. If bills show unexpected charges, a Virgo is likely to notice and address it. Some might maintain spreadsheets to track spending by category, making sure they do not spend too much on less important items. This sense of control can help them save money and meet their financial goals without feeling overwhelmed.

Conflict in Shared Living Situations

When living with family or friends, Virgos can run into conflicts if others do not share their interest in order. Simple things like leaving shoes scattered or forgetting to wipe the counters can annoy a Virgo who likes neatness. Communicating calmly is important. Instead of criticizing someone's habits, they might explain how messiness affects their sense of peace. Making small agreements—like "Shoes go in this rack" or "We clean up after cooking"—can solve many tensions. However, Virgos should also understand that nobody is perfect and that some flexibility is helpful.

Daily Tech Use

In modern life, technology is a daily part of the home. Virgos might keep their devices organized with labeled folders, regular backups, and updates. They might also set reminders or alarms on their phone for tasks. This can be a great helper if used in moderation. Yet, Virgos can also get annoyed if gadgets are slow or cluttered with unneeded apps. If they find themselves spending too much time checking messages, they might benefit from turning off notifications for a while and focusing on real-life tasks.

Personal Time and Self-Care

While Virgo likes to be useful, they also need time to recharge. Self-care activities like a warm bath, gentle stretching, or reading can help them unwind. Some Virgos find peace in quiet moments of reflection, possibly writing in a journal or simply sitting in a comfortable spot. These calm intervals let them clear their mind of daily concerns. If they do not allow time for this, they risk feeling drained and becoming overly critical of themselves or others.

Entertaining Creativity at Home

Though Virgos are practical, many still enjoy creative hobbies if they are well-structured. They might do painting with careful strokes, baking with exact measurements, or writing detailed short stories. This creative side can flourish at home, especially if they prepare a dedicated space for it. By setting up a neat corner with the right tools, they can explore their ideas without feeling like everything is scattered. This helps them relax and discover new skills they did not know they had.

Balancing Order with Comfort

One challenge for Virgos is finding a balance between neatness and coziness. A spotless house can sometimes feel too strict or cold if there are no signs of daily life. Placing comfy pillows, using soft blankets, or displaying a few personal items can make the space more welcoming. Over time, Virgos may realize that a little bit of acceptable clutter can make a home feel lived-in. Guests, friends, or family members might appreciate a house that feels warm rather than overly controlled.

Household Communication

If Virgo shares a home, clear communication keeps everything running smoothly. A Virgo might discuss chores with roommates or go over finances with a spouse. Because they love order, they can create charts or lists to track who does what. This can prevent arguments about undone chores or overlooked tasks. However, Virgos should also remain open to feedback and not insist on doing everything in their personal style. Allowing others to have input can strengthen bonds and build respect.

Emotional Maintenance at Home

Home is not just about tasks and routines; it is also the center of emotional life. A Virgo might notice subtle changes in the moods of family members. They might check in quietly, asking if someone feels stressed or tired. Offering small acts of help—like tidying a child's study desk or preparing a snack—can show care in a Virgo way. Still, they need to remember to share their own emotions, too. If they hold in worries, conflicts can build. Talking about feelings in a calm manner can prevent misunderstandings.

Long-Term Comfort and Well-Being

Over the years, a Virgo may fine-tune their living space and routines until it fits their idea of comfort. Small changes, like updating furniture for better support or rearranging shelves, can make day-to-day life smoother. They might take pride in a functional kitchen, a tidy living room, or well-managed finances. All these details serve a purpose: to create a haven where they can truly relax and feel at ease. By building and maintaining this environment, Virgos often find a sense of stability that supports their mental and emotional health.

Summary: Virgo at Home and Daily Life

In short, home is where Virgos can put their love of order to good use. Their daily routines, tidy habits, and systematic approach to tasks can make them skilled household managers. They plan meals, keep track of chores, and ensure that their space feels calm. On the flip side, they need to watch out for perfectionism and tension with others who do not share the same need for neatness. By keeping a spirit of flexibility and welcoming small comforts, Virgos can build a warm home life that nurtures their well being. They can also show their gentle care for family and friends in tangible ways, making their living space a source of calm in a busy world.

CHAPTER 11: VIRGO'S APPROACH TO PHYSICAL WELL-BEING

Overview of Virgo's Health Focus

Many Virgos care about looking after their physical health and daily habits. They often see the body as something that needs careful attention. This view can come from their wish to do things the best way possible, leading them to check labels, read tips, or plan routines. In this chapter, we will explore how Virgos handle exercise, meals, rest, and other factors that affect their bodies. We will also look at their special challenges, such as worrying too much about being perfect.

Desire for a Systematic Approach

A key trait for Virgo is their love of order. This can make them plan out their health routines carefully. They might write down a schedule for workouts or set up a meal plan for each day. Some Virgos keep a planner where they record their steps, calories, or other markers. This system helps them track progress, spot setbacks, and make changes. While other signs may rely on sudden bursts of motivation, Virgo tends to rely on consistent, methodical effort.

Studying Health Information

If a Virgo decides to improve their well-being, they often look up many details first. They could compare different diets, read up on the best exercises for their body type, or check reliable medical advice. They feel more comfortable knowing the facts before jumping into a new plan. This habit can keep them from being misled by trends. However, it can also become tiring if they overanalyze everything. Striking a balance means staying informed without getting stuck in too many details.

Daily Eating Habits

Virgos often like meal routines that are simple yet balanced. They might favor foods that give lasting energy, such as whole grains, vegetables, fruits, and lean proteins. Because they pay close attention to their own health, many prefer to avoid heavy or greasy foods. Some even keep a food diary to see how their body reacts to different meals. If they notice low energy or stomach issues, they try to adjust their meals. This precision can lead to a healthier lifestyle, though they need to watch out for overly strict habits.

Interest in Meal Prep and Cooking

When a Virgo cooks, they often enjoy the steps involved. They might measure each ingredient exactly, follow recipes closely, and adjust flavors with care. This can help them whip up tasty dishes that are also nutritious. If they have the time, they may prepare food for several days in advance, storing balanced meals in containers. This reduces stress during a busy week and helps them stick to healthy choices. However, they should also allow themselves some flexibility, so cooking does not turn into a tense task.

Exercise Patterns

Virgos are drawn to exercise methods that are structured and purposeful. Rather than random workouts, they might follow a set routine. For instance, a Virgo could schedule time for a certain type of exercise on specific days—like strength training on Mondays, a brisk walk on Wednesdays, and a gentle yoga session on Fridays. This approach matches their organized nature. Some also enjoy logging their exercise data, monitoring their improvement over time.

Enjoying Gentle Activities

Because Virgo is not typically about extreme displays of intensity, some like forms of exercise that blend movement with calm thinking, such as yoga or Pilates. These activities let them focus on the details of breathing and posture. Others might prefer going for long walks in nature, observing small sights or changes in the environment. This restful element can help them release worry and tension. It also suits their Earth sign nature, which often finds peace outdoors.

Mind-Body Connection

Virgos often recognize that emotions can affect physical well-being. If they feel upset, their body might tense up, leading to discomfort. They may try practices that join mind and body, such as controlled breathing or gentle stretches. These small moments can center them, reducing stress. Some Virgos might also keep a diary of moods and physical symptoms, looking for links that help them make better choices—like adjusting bedtime if they notice they feel better with more sleep.

Staying Motivated

One challenge for any health plan is motivation. Virgos, however, may have an advantage because they thrive on routines and structure. They see each completed workout or healthy meal as part of a well-planned system. Still, they can lose steam if they aim for unrealistic perfection. Missing a day or two might bother them more than it would others. Teaching themselves that small setbacks are normal can keep them from quitting a plan entirely.

High Standards and Stress

While a desire for good health can be positive, Virgos might put too much pressure on themselves. They could feel guilty if they skip a workout or eat a less nutritious meal. This guilt can turn a healthy goal into a stressful chore. To fight this, Virgos can remind themselves that health is a long-term journey. Slipping up sometimes is part of being human, and it does not erase the good habits they have built.

Supplements and Wellness Products

Because Virgos like to be well-informed, they might look into vitamins or herbal supplements. They want to see if these items can fill gaps in their diet or help with certain issues. While this can be helpful, they need to be careful. Not all products are tested thoroughly, and some might not be useful for their specific needs. Checking reputable sources or talking with a trusted healthcare professional is wise. This way, they avoid wasting money or risking side effects.

Concerns About Cleanliness

Some Virgos can become extra careful about germs or pollution. They might wash their hands often, keep surfaces spotless, or read product labels for potential chemicals. This caution can help them avoid illness, but it can also turn into worry if taken to extremes. Striking a healthy middle ground—like keeping clean but not panicking over every germ—helps them avoid unnecessary stress. If they notice they are becoming too fixated, it can help to talk it out or try relaxation methods.

Importance of Restful Sleep

Sleep is vital for everyone, but Virgos might especially benefit from consistent sleep routines. Because they think so much during the day, their mind can stay active at night. This makes it hard to drift off if they do not have a calming bedtime habit. Some Virgos find that reading a peaceful book, sipping herbal tea, or keeping bright screens away before bed helps them relax. Tracking bedtime and wake-up times in a planner can also help them see patterns that need adjusting.

Handling Stress and Tension

When life events pile up, Virgos can feel tense. They might hold stress in their shoulders or neck, leading to aches. Regular stretches, short breaks, or breathing exercises can lower daily strain. If stress feels overwhelming, it might help them to schedule a quick walk or a few minutes of quiet reflection. Since Virgos love order, they often respond well to a plan that includes small breaks. Even a five-minute walk can clear the mind.

Influence of Mercury

Virgo is ruled by Mercury, which is tied to thinking, speed, and nerves. This link can mean Virgos feel changes in their body quickly, such as sudden aches or tiredness, if they overdo it mentally. They might also be very aware of slight health changes. While this can be helpful for noticing early signs of an issue, it can also lead to worry. Balancing mental activity with physical grounding is key. That might include calm hobbies or time spent in nature to steady the flow of thoughts.

Setting Realistic Fitness Goals

Virgos may want to see tangible results from their exercise, such as improved strength or flexibility. However, if goals are too rigid or high, they could get discouraged when progress is slow. One tip is to set small, specific goals—for instance, adding a few extra push-ups each week or increasing walking distance by a small amount. Each mini-step can be an achievement, and that sense of progress keeps them motivated without stress.

Virgo and Alternative Health Methods

Some Virgos might explore techniques like acupuncture, reflexology, or mindfulness. Their interest usually depends on whether they see clear facts or hear trusted reviews. If a friend raves about a certain approach, Virgo might do thorough research to see if it makes sense. They are not against alternative methods, but they want to make sure they are grounded in actual benefits. Once they confirm something is safe and potentially effective, they may add it to their routine with care.

Group Workouts vs. Solo Exercise

Regarding exercise style, Virgos can go either way. Some enjoy group classes because they appreciate a set program led by an instructor who provides clear steps. Others prefer to work out alone, picking their own pace and avoiding outside pressure. The main factor is whether the environment feels structured and calm. If a gym is too crowded or loud, they might lose focus. A quiet class or a solo home workout can be more comfortable for them.

Managing Health-Related Anxiety

A tricky side of Virgo's detail-oriented mindset is that they may zero in on small physical symptoms. For example, if they feel a minor pain, they might fear it signals something serious. This worry can become a cycle: noticing something, panicking, looking up worst-case scenarios, then feeling even more worried. Talking with a doctor or a reliable health professional can ease concerns. Gathering correct data can show them that many small issues are normal and temporary.

Hygiene and Self-Care

Virgos are often known for their tidy habits. This extends to personal grooming. They might prefer routines that keep their skin clean or their hair well-tended. While self-care can be a comforting ritual, they should remain aware of slipping into perfectionism. Spending hours on grooming to correct every tiny imperfection can drain time and cause frustration. A balanced approach—ensuring good hygiene without obsessing—usually gives them the best of both worlds.

Connecting Physical and Mental Health

Virgos often recognize that emotional well-being and physical health are tied. A rough day can make them skip a workout or crave comfort foods. If they see these links, they can adjust gently. Maybe they plan a calmer workout after a long workday or pick a healthier snack that still feels comforting. By addressing their feelings, they can keep their overall health goals on track. This rounded view of health prevents them from separating the body and mind as if they are unrelated.

Handling Setbacks

It is common for people to face setbacks in a health routine—an injury, a busy period at work, or a general loss of motivation. For Virgos, this can feel extra tough because they like to keep everything in neat order. They might blame themselves or think, "I failed." The best remedy is to remember that small disruptions happen to everyone. Creating a plan to return slowly—like starting with easy exercises or adjusting meal plans—can help them feel in control again. Patience is key, because pushing too hard too soon might lead to more problems.

Body Positivity and Self-Acceptance

Virgos may focus so strongly on improvement that they forget to appreciate what is already good about their bodies. They might fixate on a certain look or a certain weight. A healthier view would be to honor the strengths they have, such as endurance, flexibility, or a balanced meal plan. By recognizing each positive step, they lower the risk of feeling critical about themselves. Self-acceptance does not mean ignoring goals; it means valuing who they are, even as they make adjustments.

Building a Support Network

A Virgo who is serious about health can benefit from supportive friends or family. They might discuss recipes, share exercise ideas, or go on walks together. This social support can keep them motivated and give them a break from always pushing themselves alone. It also helps if the people around them understand their logical side and do not tease them for being thorough. When a Virgo feels accepted, they are more likely to keep up healthy habits.

Exploring Calmness and Relaxation

Because Virgos can overthink or feel anxious, planning relaxation into their routines is helpful. This can include breathing exercises, slow stretches, a simple meditation app, or peaceful walks in nature. Some enjoy mild music or soothing sounds. The key is to find an activity that truly calms them. These small breaks can reduce the strain that builds up from daily tasks. Over time, they learn that caring for their mental state also gives them better physical outcomes, like lower stress and more stable energy levels.

Avoiding Over-Analysis

While Virgo's skill in details can be a gift, it might also lead them to place too much importance on health data. They could keep comparing themselves to others or checking minor changes in weight or muscle tone. This can suck the fun out of staying fit and turn it into a numbers game. Letting go of constant measuring and enjoying an activity for its own sake—like dancing or walking with a friend—allows them to stay healthy without feeling locked into data reports.

Simple Reminders for Virgo's Well-Being

Stay Balanced: Aim for healthy routines, but leave room for a little flexibility.

Learn the Basics: Focus on the main parts of health—consistent exercise, balanced meals, plenty of rest, and stress control—rather than chasing after every new idea.

Set Clear, Small Goals: Writing down short targets can be more encouraging than trying to jump straight to a major outcome.

Ask for Support: Share goals with a friend or a trainer if that helps you stay on track.

Celebrate Small Wins: Recognize daily progress, such as doing a few more reps or choosing a healthy meal when busy.

Wrapping Up Virgo's Physical Health Perspective
Virgos approach physical well-being with organization, care, and methodical effort. They like to plan workouts, keep track of meal choices, and stay updated on medical information. All this helps

them maintain a strong and balanced body. The main pitfall is being too self-critical or aiming for extremes. By allowing for imperfections and learning to relax, Virgos can continue to improve their health while keeping a calm mind. Their skill at noticing changes and planning routines can guide them toward a stable sense of well-being in the long run.

Final Thoughts

Virgos thrive when they see health as a blend of consistent actions, informed choices, and gentle self-acceptance. Their knack for detail can be a wonderful ally, as long as they do not let it turn into unhealthy stress. By focusing on balance, realistic goals, and enjoying the process, Virgo can maintain a healthy body and a peaceful spirit. This approach also benefits the people around them, as Virgos often share tips and help others stick to better habits. In the end, it is about living in a way that respects their inner need for order while still welcoming a bit of flexibility.

CHAPTER 12: VIRGO AND PERSONAL DEVELOPMENT

Understanding Virgo's Need to Grow

Personal development often means learning and improving skills, habits, or one's outlook on life. For Virgos, this is a natural area of focus. They usually see progress as an ongoing task. Because they are detail-oriented and practical, they may look for methods to boost their knowledge, refine behavior, or become more efficient. In this chapter, we will look at how Virgos tackle self-improvement in daily life, along with ways they can keep a healthy balance and not get lost in strict perfectionism.

Link to Mercury and Analytical Thinking

Virgo is ruled by Mercury, which is associated with thinking, communication, and the urge to gather facts. This can make Virgos curious, always looking for new information that can help them advance. They might read books or articles, watch videos, or talk with experts. If a topic sparks their interest—like psychology, a new software, or a skill—they might research in depth before trying it out. This tendency supports their development, since they rarely jump into something blindly.

Setting Practical Goals

One major way Virgos enhance themselves is through goal-setting. Instead of vague statements like "I want to be better," they often specify targets such as:

"Learn a new language up to a certain level of fluency."

"Get a certificate in a field that interests me."

"Improve my public speaking by practicing once a week."

They write down each goal in detail, noting steps or milestones along the way. For Virgo, having a clear map to follow is both comforting and motivating. They enjoy ticking items off a checklist or seeing consistent progress.

Managing Self-Criticism

While aiming to improve can be positive, it can turn harsh if Virgos become too self-critical. If they set high standards, they may notice every small slip. For example, if they plan to learn an instrument and miss a few notes, they might feel they are not making progress fast enough. Over time, this strict self-judgment can drain their excitement. A more relaxed view can help them see that steady growth includes errors. Each mistake can be a stepping stone rather than a sign of failure.

Enjoyment in Learning

Despite the caution above, Virgos often love the process of gaining knowledge. They might go through tutorials step by step, take notes, and then practice thoroughly. For them, the act of learning can be satisfying because it feeds their need for mental order. Learning also keeps them from feeling stuck in routine. When they pick a topic that truly interests them—like cooking, coding, painting, or a musical instrument—they can become quite skilled over time.

Applying Skills in Real Life

Virgos usually like to put their abilities into practice. They might learn a new software and then use it to manage tasks at work more efficiently. If they study cooking techniques, they will likely test them in the kitchen, adjusting flavors until they are happy. This hands-on approach ensures that knowledge turns into tangible results. They do not just want to collect facts; they want to see a difference in their day-to-day life.

Balancing Many Interests

Because Virgos can be curious, they might have multiple projects going at once—learning a language, trying a craft, reading self-improvement books, etc. The risk is spreading themselves too thin. If they start five new courses at the same time, they might not have enough energy or time to do any of them deeply. Virgo can avoid burnout by picking one or two main goals to focus on, leaving other interests on hold. This approach leads to stronger progress and prevents them from feeling overwhelmed.

Organizing the Development Process

Virgos are known for their organizational skills. They might create a structured plan for personal growth, using a spreadsheet or planner. For instance, they can schedule daily practice, weekly reflections, and monthly tests of what they have learned. This method helps them avoid drifting, which can happen if they rely purely on inspiration. By treating self-improvement like a series of small tasks, they build momentum day after day.

Learning from Mistakes

Since Virgos pay attention to small errors, they can be good at spotting what went wrong. They may replay a situation in their mind—like a messy social interaction or a project that failed—and pick out the key mistakes. As long as they do not get stuck in regret, this review can be useful. They can note what to change next time. For example, if they tried to speak up in a group but ended up feeling flustered, they might practice short, clear talking points ahead of the next meeting.

Seeking Help and Mentors

Virgos might also look for people who can guide them—mentors, teachers, or skilled friends. Because Virgos respect expertise, they appreciate receiving structured tips from someone with experience. They usually show up prepared, with questions ready and a notebook to record advice. They aim to use each session effectively, reflecting their wish not to waste time. This can lead them to form strong mentor-mentee bonds, as they show real commitment to the process.

Handling Self-Doubt

As Virgos focus on growth, they might face periods of doubt. They may wonder if they have chosen the right path or if they are capable enough. This doubt can grow if they see others who seem more advanced or if they do not see fast results. One way to handle this is to remember that personal advancement is unique for each person. Another is to track small achievements. Seeing how far they have come, even in minor steps, can restore motivation.

Emotional Growth and Empathy

Personal advancement is not just about knowledge or skills. Virgos can also aim to become kinder, more patient, or more understanding. They might read about emotional skills—like managing anger or listening better. Once they learn strategies, they try them out in real-life settings. For example, if they notice a friend is upset, they apply active listening techniques. Over time, these efforts can help them build warmer, more supportive relationships. The key is to avoid turning emotional growth into a strict checklist. Feelings also need a natural flow.

Experiencing Fun During Growth

Virgos can sometimes get too serious when trying to improve themselves. They might see personal development as one more job. If they take that approach for too long, it could remove the joy that comes from new discoveries. Allowing a bit of fun—like learning a skill just because it is interesting, not because it is "useful"—can lighten their perspective. Trying something silly or out of their comfort zone can also help them loosen up. That sense of play often fuels creativity and new insights.

Avoiding Comparison

In the age of social media, people often compare themselves to what others show online. Virgos may be at risk of feeling inadequate if they see someone else's perfect achievements. It is important to remember that not everyone shares their full struggles. Personal growth moves at different speeds for different people. A Virgo might find it more fulfilling to compare their current self to their past self, rather than measuring themselves against others. This type of self-comparison can show real progress and encourage them to keep going.

Building Steady Confidence

Virgos often value practical proof of progress. Whenever they finish a course or master a new skill, it can boost their confidence in a genuine way. They know they put in the work, and the results are visible. Over time, they become more comfortable trying challenging tasks because they trust their ability to learn. This confidence is not loud or boastful, but rather a quiet belief that if they follow the right steps, they can adapt and improve.

Time Management

Balancing personal growth with daily responsibilities can be tricky. Virgos might have a job, family duties, and social commitments, so they need to fit their self-improvement tasks into the schedule. Because they excel at planning, they might block off short periods each day—like 20 minutes of language study in the morning or a half-hour of reading at night. By keeping these time blocks modest, they ensure they do not burn out. Gradually, these small chunks of effort add up to impressive results.

Finding Accountability

Sometimes, Virgos benefit from having someone hold them accountable. This could be a friend who also wants to learn a skill, a study group, or an online forum. If they know they have to report their progress, they are more likely to stick to their plan. Sharing small wins can also create motivation and keep them from feeling isolated in their efforts. However, Virgos might need to be careful not to judge themselves harshly if they see others moving faster.

Practical Tools for Self-Reflection

Many Virgos enjoy written methods for tracking their thoughts and progress. Keeping a journal of daily ups and downs, listing goals, and noting any key lessons can be very helpful. They might review these notes weekly or monthly, observing patterns. This method can reveal that times of slow progress or frustration often lead to learning. Reflecting in writing also helps them think more clearly about what they want and how to get there.

Positive Reinforcement

Encouragement is crucial. Virgos might be used to spotting mistakes, so they need regular reminders that they are doing well. If they reach a milestone—like finishing a challenging chapter in a textbook or completing a personal project—they should pause to acknowledge that step. Even a small treat, a short break, or a kind word to themselves can keep them on track. Over time, these positive notes counterbalance their natural tendency toward self-criticism.

Handling Plateaus

In personal growth, plateaus happen when progress seems to stall. A Virgo might learn a lot at first, then feel stuck. This can trigger worry or push them to quit. Instead, they can view a plateau as a time to refine what they have learned. Maybe they need to revisit the basics or seek fresh methods. For example, if they are learning a language and feel they are not improving, they might try speaking with a tutor or switch to new materials. Plateaus can be catalysts for trying new approaches.

Motivation During Busy Times

Sometimes life throws curveballs—deadlines at work, changes at home, or health concerns. During these periods, Virgos might not have the energy to push forward in their personal goals. Instead of feeling guilty, they can reduce expectations until things settle. They might move from a daily practice to a weekly practice or pick smaller, more relaxed tasks. Keeping a light presence in their self-improvement efforts helps them maintain a connection to their goals without adding stress.

Embracing Imperfection

A central lesson for Virgos is learning that personal development does not mean eliminating all flaws. Everyone has weaknesses, and life is not always tidy. Sometimes, being flexible or accepting that events may go in unexpected directions is its own form of growth. A Virgo could gain more from practicing patience or compassion than from chasing a rigid idea of "perfect." In fact, letting go of the idea of perfect can open the door to greater creativity and joy.

Sharing Knowledge with Others

When Virgos develop a new skill, they often want to help others learn it too. They might teach friends, join a community class, or write guides. This sharing can deepen their understanding and sharpen their ability to explain concepts. It also feels satisfying to pass on what they have gained. However, they need to avoid being too critical of people who learn at a slower pace or use different methods. Patience and empathy go a long way toward making them helpful teachers.

Broadening Horizons

Personal development can also mean stepping outside familiar territory. If a Virgo always focuses on logic or structure, it might help them to try creative or abstract pursuits. Maybe they take up painting without worrying about precision, or they explore a musical style that seems unusual. These experiences can expand their perspective, showing them that not all growth can be planned out neatly. Embracing some randomness can foster fresh inspiration and reduce the urge to control everything.

Aligning Growth with Values

Virgos often have strong moral or ethical principles. Linking personal growth to these values can bring extra meaning. For instance, they might learn communication skills so they can help local groups or volunteer. They might pick up organizational strategies and use them to support a charity or a good cause. When their progress aligns with something they care about deeply, it fuels their motivation and creates a sense of purpose. They feel that each new skill or insight is also helping the world around them.

Staying Flexible

Over time, a Virgo may notice that what worked in the past is not as effective now. They might discover that a study schedule they used five years ago no longer fits their current life. Accepting these changes can prevent frustration. By staying flexible and revising their approach, Virgos keep personal growth fresh. They see that each stage of life might call for a different style of learning, a different pace, or a different focus.

Long-Term Outlook

For Virgo, personal development is not a single event. It is more like an ongoing process, which suits their mindset of constant improvement. They might try new courses, read new books, or refine their approach to daily tasks throughout their entire life. This steady approach, driven by curiosity and a wish to do better, often leads Virgos to become dependable, knowledgeable individuals who can adapt to many changes over time. They also become good advisors for friends or family members who are seeking reliable tips for learning and growth.

Self-Compassion as a Key

If there is one area that helps Virgos thrive, it is learning to be kind to themselves. Without self-compassion, personal growth can turn into a harsh treadmill of always trying to fix every flaw. By speaking gently to themselves and viewing mistakes as normal, Virgos can stay resilient. This self-kindness offers a stable base for all the new skills or insights they hope to gain. It also helps them remain patient with others who might not share the same drive or style.

Connecting with the Bigger Picture

While Virgos are grounded in day-to-day details, they also benefit from stepping back to see the bigger picture. They can ask: "How does this goal fit into my life as a whole?" or "Will this skill add real value to the person I want to be?" Questions like these prevent them from getting lost in tiny tasks that do not serve a larger aim. They remind the Virgo that personal growth is about building a fulfilling life, not just checking off boxes on a chart.

CHAPTER 13: VIRGO COMMUNICATION STYLES

Virgos often communicate in a calm and organized way. They tend to think before they speak, picking their words carefully so they say exactly what they mean. This approach can make them appear reserved at times, but it also shows that they value clarity. Some Virgos may even jot down notes before an important call or conversation. This habit allows them to feel prepared, ensuring they do not leave out crucial points or forget what they want to say.

Because Virgos are detail-focused, they can be skilled at explaining complex topics step by step. They might break an idea into smaller parts, giving examples along the way. This style can be very helpful when they are training someone at work or explaining instructions to a friend. However, they must watch for moments when others might not need so much detail. Some people prefer a quick summary, so knowing when to be concise is also part of good communication.

Listening is another side of Virgo's communication strength. Many Virgos are good listeners who pay attention to both the words and the tone being used. If a friend is upset, Virgo may pick up on small clues in their voice or choice of words. This helps Virgo respond more thoughtfully. However, they might pause before offering a reply, as they want to gather all the facts. In fast-paced discussions, they could be seen as shy or hesitant, though they are simply being cautious.

In everyday talk, Virgos often prefer direct language. They do not like to pile on fancy or confusing terms. Instead, they lean toward clear and straightforward phrases. This can be a relief to people who prefer no-nonsense speech. But in some social settings, others might view Virgos as too serious. When having fun with friends, Virgos can try adding light humor or personal remarks to show warmth. Balancing simple clarity with a friendly tone can help them connect more easily.

Virgos might also be mindful about body language. When speaking, they could keep a relaxed posture or maintain steady eye contact to show that they are paying attention. They might nod to signal that they understand or that they want the other person to continue talking. Because they are detail-oriented, they notice subtle cues—like a shift in someone's expression or posture. This awareness makes them good at sensing tension or discomfort. However, they have to remember not to overthink every glance or gesture.

Written communication is another area where Virgos may shine. They tend to write in a structured manner, using clear sentences and well-organized paragraphs. Whether it is a quick note, a text message, or a longer email, they usually proofread for errors. They do not like the idea of sending out sloppy work. This caution helps them present ideas more effectively. On the downside, some Virgos may spend too long perfecting their messages, turning simple emails into lengthy tasks.

When working in a group, Virgo may take on the role of the person who keeps everything on track. They might send reminders or create lists so everyone knows the plan. Their updates might be very clear about what has been done and what remains. Others on the team can appreciate this structure, though they might also joke that Virgo is "too organized." Striking the right balance is key. Virgos benefit the group by being meticulous, but they should also give teammates space for their own styles.

Conflict resolution can be tricky. Virgos often want to solve the issue by discussing facts and steps to fix it. They might lay out evidence and point to specific times or words used in the conflict. This can be useful, yet it might frustrate someone who is led by feelings. Virgos can learn that acknowledging emotions can be just as important as stating facts. A simple phrase like, "I understand how you feel," can open the door to better outcomes.

Virgos appreciate honesty in others. If they sense a hint of dishonesty or vague language, they may try asking follow-up questions. In some cases, they might come across as interrogating the other person, though that is rarely their intention. They simply want to understand. If their questions become too numerous, it can strain the conversation. Learning to recognize when to accept an answer without endless digging can help keep interactions friendlier.

In romantic relationships, Virgo's communication style often involves practical tips and care. They might not shower a partner with flowery words, but they could show concern by asking about daily tasks or offering small assistance. The Virgo partner might say, "Have you eaten yet?" or "Don't forget to rest if you're tired." It might seem routine, but it is a sign of real care. Over time, some partners wish for more warm or emotional words, so Virgos can try mixing in gentle expressions of affection.

Among friends, Virgos can be the ones who give thorough, thoughtful advice. Because they notice small details, they can point out aspects others have missed. At times, though, this can sound like they are being too critical. If a friend vents about a problem, Virgo might respond with a list of steps or possible solutions. Not everyone wants a "fix." Some just want a listening ear. Learning to ask, "Do you want my thoughts or do you just want me to listen?" can prevent misunderstandings.

Humor is a less obvious side of Virgo. They can be witty observers, noticing silly things in daily life. Their jokes might come from small details no one else saw. However, they might not always share these jokes out loud, worried about how others will react. With close friends, Virgo can feel safe enough to drop their guard, and their humor can be surprisingly sharp. Letting this side show more often can help them build social ease and stronger bonds.

When presenting in public, Virgos often prepare thoroughly. They might rehearse in front of a mirror or write an outline in detail. Their speech tends to be structured, with a clear beginning, middle, and end. They may use supporting facts or examples, especially if the topic is complex. This approach can make them reliable presenters who rarely go off-topic. Still, they might feel nervous about slipping up. Understanding that a small pause or minor error is normal can free them to speak more naturally.

Virgos often enjoy technology-based communication, such as emails or texts, because it allows them time to craft a clear response. They might find phone calls slightly more tense, as they have to think on the spot. Videoconferences can also be a mixed experience: Virgo might like seeing the person's face but can feel self-conscious about their own background or appearance. Taking a moment to set things up neatly before a call can help them feel more at ease.

Another feature of Virgo's style is that they might prefer to keep private matters out of casual chats. They can be friendly but guarded. If someone asks a personal question, Virgo may respond with only the needed details. They do not typically overshare. This can protect them from feeling exposed, but it might mean people view them as distant. Over time, as trust grows, they might open up more. A friend who sticks around will see that Virgos have plenty of thoughts and feelings.

Virgos may also be sensitive to how others phrase things. A small hint of sarcasm or a critical tone can linger in their mind. They might analyze whether the person was serious or joking. This can lead them to double-check the meaning of certain remarks. If a friend or coworker is direct or blunt, Virgo might feel uneasy at first. With time, they can learn to distinguish between someone being harsh and someone simply speaking plainly.

When it comes to giving feedback, Virgos usually try to be constructive. They might say, "I think you did really well on this part, and maybe we could adjust that part for clarity." This helps the other person see that there is good in their effort, as well as room to grow. The downside is that Virgos might give more suggestions than a person expects. If they sense the other person feels overwhelmed, it can help to focus on only one or two main tips at a time.

In group conversations, Virgos can appear quiet, especially if the topic is something they know little about. They prefer not to speak just for the sake of speaking. Instead, they observe. If they have something meaningful to add, they will do so in a well-thought-out way. Some might perceive this as shyness, but many Virgos simply choose their moments. When they do speak, it often adds depth to the discussion, because they have been analyzing the topic.

If Virgos sense tension or negative feelings in the air, they might try to smooth things over with a practical suggestion. They could say, "Let's list what needs to be done so we can move forward," or "How about we clarify each person's role so no one feels left out?" Their approach is to solve the source of conflict with a plan. But if the issue is more emotional, they might need to step back and let others express their feelings before offering a plan.

Virgos also value timeliness in communication. If they expect an answer from someone, they can grow uneasy when that answer is late or vague. Likewise, they strive to reply promptly themselves, especially in professional contexts. In personal conversations, they might not always message back instantly, but they do not like leaving people waiting too long. This sense of responsibility can be appreciated by those who prefer quick responses, though it can cause Virgo to feel pressured if they are busy.

Tone of voice can matter a lot to Virgo. They often speak in a steady tone, which can sound soothing. On the other hand, if they are upset or frustrated, the difference might show in a sharper tone, even if they do not raise their voice. Others who know them well can pick up on this shift right away. Because Virgos prefer calm interactions, they might retreat if someone yells or uses an aggressive tone. A gentler discussion is more in line with their communication comfort.

Sarcasm and teasing can be tricky. Some Virgos dislike sarcasm because it feels indirect or mean. They prefer straightforward remarks that clearly show if the speaker is serious or joking. If a friend teases them too often, Virgo might interpret it as genuine criticism. Learning to see harmless teasing for what it is can help them relax. At the same time, friends who value Virgo's feelings might try to use warmer, more open humor around them.

When it comes to giving instructions, Virgos often break them down into steps. They might say, "First do this, next do that, then check this." They want to ensure that nothing is overlooked. This can be great for teaching new skills, but some might find it too rigid if they already have a sense of how to proceed. Reading the listener's level of experience helps Virgo adjust the depth of their explanation.

If Virgos find themselves in a misunderstanding, they might attempt to fix it by reviewing exactly what was said or written. They might say, "On Monday, I used these words, and I think you heard something else." This detailed method can clear up confusion, but it can also feel like a "play-by-play" that some find tedious. Balancing thoroughness with an understanding of emotional nuance is crucial.

A quick "I'm sorry, let's move past it" may be enough if the other person is not looking for a deep analysis.

In conclusion, Virgo communication styles combine clarity, thoughtfulness, and a preference for well-structured dialogue. They do well when given time to gather their ideas, often expressing them with precision. They also listen carefully, spotting subtle signals from others. At their best, Virgos bring order and reason to conversations, helping people cover all important details. The main challenge is learning to handle emotions—both their own and others'—with the same level of care. By blending empathy with their logical strengths, Virgos can form lasting bonds and communicate effectively in all kinds of situations.

CHAPTER 14: VIRGO'S RELATIONSHIP WITH FINANCES

Money can be a source of both comfort and stress, and Virgos tend to approach finances with care and organization. Whether it is about saving, spending, or investing, Virgos often like having a plan in place. This chapter explores how Virgo's traits shape their money habits, what they value financially, and where they might struggle. By understanding these patterns, Virgos can make wiser decisions and reduce financial worries.

One hallmark of Virgo's approach to money is the wish for stability. They often like to know that they have a solid cushion of savings in case of emergencies. This might mean they start saving early in life, even if it is just small amounts. They might also look for a reliable form of income rather than jumping into risky ventures. The idea of having a backup plan appeals to their practical side, giving them peace of mind in a changing world.

Another trait is attention to detail. When it comes to budgeting, Virgos can be quite thorough. They might make a spreadsheet or use an app to track every expense. This habit helps them notice spending patterns—like how much goes toward daily coffee or a hobby. Knowing exactly where their money goes allows them to plan better. However, some Virgos might become too fixated on tiny differences, leading them to feel stressed if the budget does not match perfectly each month.

Virgos often prefer a neat financial record. They may keep receipts filed in chronological order, label envelopes for different bills, or set reminders on their phone to pay everything on time. This prevents missed deadlines and late fees. Being on top of due dates is part of their desire for order. It also keeps them from feeling anxious about forgetting a payment. However, if they live with people who are more relaxed about finances, conflicts could arise over what they see as a careless attitude.

Spending style can vary among Virgos, but a common thread is that they usually think before making purchases. Impulse buying is less likely, unless something truly appeals to their sense of practicality. For instance, they might buy a tool if it can help them do tasks more efficiently. Or they might invest in a well-made piece of furniture that lasts longer. They tend to view quality as a good reason to spend more, believing it will save money in the long run.

Even though Virgos are cautious, they are not always stingy. If they see value in something—like a gift for a loved one or a home improvement that will bring comfort—they might be willing to spend. But they usually do so with research, comparing prices or reading reviews to ensure they are making a good choice. They do not like wasting money on poorly made items. This approach can lead to fewer regrets about purchases, as they have done their homework ahead of time.

When it comes to saving, Virgos often set aside a part of their paycheck regularly. They might open different savings accounts for specific goals, such as travel, a home project, or future education. This labeling can motivate them to save more, as they see the balance growing for each goal. However, if unexpected costs arise, Virgos might feel uneasy tapping into those funds. They might view it as messing with their carefully planned system.

Investing is another area where Virgos can do well, provided they do enough research. They might look into mutual funds, stocks, or bonds, reading up on the risks before committing. Their logical approach and dislike of sudden moves can keep them from falling for quick-profit schemes. Still, they may sometimes be too hesitant, missing chances to invest earlier or in options that carry slightly higher risk but better returns. Striking a balance between safety and growth can help them see long-term benefits.

Budgeting apps or other tech tools can suit Virgo's methodical style. They might enjoy inputting transactions, generating charts, and analyzing trends. This process satisfies their interest in data, letting them see month-to-month progress. If they notice rising costs in a certain category, they can adjust sooner. The challenge is not to become overly consumed by the numbers. Checking a budget daily can be helpful, but living in constant worry over small changes might bring unnecessary stress.

Debt is something Virgos usually try to avoid. They do not like the idea of owing money if they can help it. As a result, many Virgos prefer to pay with cash or pay off credit card balances in full each month. This practice can keep them out of trouble, but sometimes big life events—like buying a home—require taking on a loan. In those cases, Virgos will often plan a schedule to pay extra toward the principal, cutting interest costs. It can feel reassuring to see the debt shrink predictably.

If they have a partner, Virgos want clarity on shared finances. They might suggest combining certain expenses while keeping individual accounts for personal spending. Or they might propose a system where each person contributes a set amount to a joint fund. Communication is key: Virgos want to avoid hidden costs or messy arguments about who owes what. By setting clear rules, they reduce tension. However, they also have to be open to a partner's different style if that partner is more relaxed or spontaneous with money.

In families, Virgo might take charge of organizing money matters. They could handle paying bills, scheduling repairs, or comparing deals for utilities. Others often trust them because they are thorough and reliable. Yet, Virgo must guard against feeling they must do it all. If they handle every financial task alone, they could become stressed. Sharing some tasks with responsible family members can free them to focus on what truly needs their detail-oriented mind.

One area where Virgos might stumble is overthinking about future risks. They could worry about losing their job, unexpected medical bills, or large home repairs. While a certain amount of planning is good, too much worry can affect their peace of mind. They might over-save, neglecting simple pleasures. It is helpful for Virgos to remind themselves that small joys or experiences can be worth the cost, as long as they keep their main savings plan intact.

Generosity can show up in subtle ways. Virgos might offer financial help to a friend in trouble, but they do not usually broadcast it. They prefer quiet forms of support, such as giving a relative a loan to start a small business or quietly covering a friend's meal if they are short on funds. They might not be the type to donate large sums without research. Instead, they check how the money will be used, ensuring it goes to a trustworthy cause. This aligns with their practical approach to giving.

Workplace earnings can be a focus for Virgos, but they are often not the type to chase huge salaries at all costs. They want fair pay for honest work, valuing steady growth over dramatic leaps. If they see a chance to learn new skills and earn more responsibly, they might pursue it. Still, they might avoid jobs that seem unstable, even if the pay is higher. Their sense of caution leans them toward positions where they can build a stable record of income.

Negotiating can be a challenge. Virgos tend to be polite and may not push aggressively for raises or better deals. They prefer calm discussions backed by facts—like their accomplishments or the market rates for their role. If the other side is forceful, a Virgo might feel uneasy. In such cases, coming prepared with data can help them stand their ground. Learning to speak confidently about their own worth can lead to fair compensation, which supports their broader financial goals.

When it comes to managing daily spending, Virgos often keep an eye out for sales or discounts that make sense. They might clip coupons or wait for off-season prices on items they need. However, they rarely fall for a discount just because it is there. They still ask, "Do I really need this?" or "Is this brand reliable?" This thoughtful approach can help them save money without cluttering the house with bargains that never get used.

Virgos might enjoy do-it-yourself (DIY) tasks if it can save money in a practical way. For example, they might fix minor home issues themselves or mend clothing to avoid new purchases. This combines their detail-oriented nature with financial caution. However, they must make sure not to tackle projects that are too large or risky, which might cost more to fix later. Knowing when professional help is needed prevents them from spending unnecessary money on redoing mistakes.

Social events that involve shared expenses can be a source of confusion if the group does not define who pays what. Virgos might propose splitting the bill in a fair manner or itemizing each person's order to avoid misunderstandings. While some friends might find this approach overly precise, it is Virgo's way of ensuring no one feels cheated. They are not trying to be cheap; they just believe that clarity is the best path to harmony.

Virgos in creative fields might sometimes doubt if their art or craft will provide a stable income. This concern can prompt them to keep a side job or remain in a traditional job until they feel safe to rely on their creative work. While caution is helpful, they should also allow room for growth in their chosen field. A careful plan—like saving extra money while building a portfolio—can ease fears. Slowly, they might find the balance between security and following a creative passion.

Retirement planning can start early for Virgo. They might research different retirement accounts or talk to financial advisors for guidance. They see the logic in preparing for later years rather than leaving it to chance. By setting regular contributions, they reduce the stress of wondering whether they will have enough in old age. Once again, the potential pitfall is overthinking. It is good to remember that retirement should also include some enjoyment. If they put aside too much, they might miss out on experiences in the present.

When faced with financial setbacks, Virgos can turn to their planning skills. If a job loss or medical expense arises, they look for ways to adjust. They might cut back on optional spending, find part-time work to cover bills, or temporarily move some savings around. Their organized nature can help them respond calmly, but they must also be careful not to panic over every dip. Recognizing that ups and downs happen in life can help them stay level-headed.

Virgos benefit from setting realistic money goals rather than aiming for extremes. For instance, deciding to save a set amount each month for a year can be more effective than trying to stash every extra dollar. It's also wise to build in a small "fun" budget, so they do not feel guilty about occasional treats. This approach keeps them motivated and avoids a sense of constant sacrifice. Over time, consistent, moderate saving often beats sporadic bursts of extreme frugality.

Learning from mistakes is part of a healthy financial path. Virgos might recall a time they overspent or invested poorly. Instead of denying it, they can analyze the event. What signs did they ignore? Which research did they skip? By reviewing errors, they refine their approach. This helps them grow wiser about money without beating themselves up. After all, everyone slips up sometimes, and turning those moments into lessons can prevent bigger errors later.

In summary, Virgos often handle finances with caution, methodical planning, and a preference for clear systems. They track expenses, avoid reckless debt, and aim to save for the future. They can be generous in quiet ways, though they rarely make large decisions without thorough thought. The risk lies in over-worrying or becoming too rigid. By staying open to some flexibility, allowing themselves small pleasures, and balancing risk and safety, Virgos can enjoy both security and the rewards of their hard work. This measured approach to money helps them build a stable foundation for themselves and the people they care about.

Overall, Virgos thrive when they treat finances as a steady process of growth, rather than a scramble to grab every opportunity. Their detail-oriented mindset can keep them safe from hasty actions, and their sense of responsibility can help them move forward at a pace that feels right. By blending caution with a bit of boldness now and then, they can see their resources develop over time. In the end, money becomes a tool for comfort and security, rather than a source of ongoing worry.

CHAPTER 15: INTERESTS AND PASTIMES FOR VIRGO

Virgos have a natural sense of care and thoroughness, and these traits often shape what they do in their free time. While everyone is different, many people born under Virgo lean toward hobbies and interests that let them see clear results or improvements. Because they like to be useful and productive, they tend to pick pastimes that give them a feeling of accomplishment. This chapter explores possible activities that suit Virgo's style, how they manage these hobbies, and the unique enjoyment and potential hurdles that come with each choice.

Enjoyment of Orderly Tasks

A number of Virgos enjoy activities that bring order or clarity. This might mean something like solving puzzles, sorting collectibles, or creating a system for storing items in the house. While some people see these tasks as chores, Virgos might see them as pleasant ways to relax. For example, sorting through old photos and arranging them in a neat album can be soothing because it involves setting up a clear sequence. Virgo's eye for detail makes them notice small issues, like a mislabeled picture or a gap in the timeline. By correcting these things, they feel a sense of completion.

Similarly, organizing digital files can be a pastime for some Virgos. They might label folders by date or subject, making it easy to find important documents. This process can be oddly comforting because it reduces clutter and keeps everything in the right place.

Virgos may also like helping friends or family tidy up their spaces, if asked. They get to use their practical skills and see a visible transformation. However, they should watch out for taking on too many of these tasks, as constant organizing can become tiring if it stops feeling like a fun pastime.

Learning-Based Hobbies

Many Virgos enjoy picking up new knowledge in their free time. This could mean reading non-fiction books about a topic they find interesting, watching online lectures, or practicing a language. Because Mercury is linked to Virgo, they often find mental stimulation rewarding. They may take detailed notes as they study, storing them neatly so they can refer back later. This methodical approach helps them absorb the information step by step.

In some cases, Virgos might use apps or websites that track daily progress in a skill. For instance, a language-learning platform might give them a short lesson each day, building consistency. This structure satisfies Virgo's liking for routines. They can see exactly what they covered, how many words they learned, and which exercises they need to review. Over time, they build a solid foundation of knowledge. This process can be more enjoyable for a Virgo than spontaneous learning, because they like seeing clear milestones and feeling steady improvement.

Another learning-based pastime could be exploring technical skills, such as coding, design, or editing software. Virgos appreciate tasks that have a logical pattern. For instance, coding requires a step-by-step mindset: you write instructions, test them, find errors, and fix them. The same is true for design tasks, where you might adjust shapes or colors until they are just right. Virgo's knack for detail can turn these pursuits into a gratifying hobby, allowing them to refine their abilities a bit each day.

Gardening and Nature-Related Activities

As an Earth sign, Virgo often feels at ease doing things related to nature. Gardening is a common pastime that suits their patient and nurturing side. Planting seeds, caring for them, and watching them grow can be very satisfying. Virgos may enjoy reading about soil conditions, watering schedules, and best planting times. Then they apply these tips carefully, adjusting as they see results. It is a down-to-earth hobby that blends structure (planning what to plant and when) with hands-on care.

In a similar way, Virgos might like nature walks or hikes. Instead of rushing, they might pay attention to small details, like how certain leaves are shaped or which birds are calling in the distance. They could keep a small notebook, jotting down what they see or learn. This approach turns a simple walk into a purposeful outing, tapping into Virgo's interest in gathering information. However, they must remember to take breaks and not make it all about collecting data, or it might start to feel more like work than leisure.

Some Virgos also extend their attention to caring for pets or animals in need. Volunteering at an animal shelter or fostering a pet can bring them joy. They find satisfaction in helping living beings thrive. Because they are observant, they might notice small changes in an animal's behavior or health, stepping in with help or advice. Balancing this volunteer activity with other daily responsibilities is important, so they do not get overwhelmed. Still, many Virgos find it a heartwarming way to spend free time.

Crafting, DIY Projects, and Creative Outlets

Virgos can be creative, but they often like art forms that rely on planning or technique. For example, knitting, crocheting, or sewing can appeal because they involve patterns, careful counting, and visible progress. A Virgo might follow a detailed design, checking each row or stitch. They enjoy seeing the final product become something functional, like a scarf or a sweater. This sense of structure within creativity strikes a balance that fits Virgo well.

DIY home projects, such as minor repairs, painting rooms, or building simple furniture, also attract some Virgos. They like the idea of improving their environment, and their methodical side comes in handy for measuring, cutting, and following instructions. Each step is tackled in an orderly way—gathering materials, laying out the plan, and moving step by step until it is done. Again, the result is visible and practical. Virgos must only be careful not to take on too big of a project if they lack the time or expertise, as that can lead to frustration and unfinished tasks.

Writing or journaling can be another creative outlet. While some might assume Virgos only write academic or factual pieces, many Virgos also enjoy personal expression in the form of poetry or short stories. They might craft carefully worded lines, editing multiple times to capture the exact mood or message. Others might keep a journal to note daily events, insights, or lists. Having a record of thoughts can feel orderly, giving them something to look back on for reflection or self-awareness.

Cooking and Baking

Cooking can be an enjoyable pastime for Virgo. It involves planning, measuring, and following steps, all of which fit a Virgo's systematic approach. They might collect recipes, experiment with small changes, and keep notes on what worked best. Over time, they build a personal cookbook that is precise and reliable. The reward is a tasty meal, which can also be shared with friends or family. Virgo's practical nature means they often enjoy cooking dishes that are both healthy and flavorful, bringing the best of both worlds.

Baking, in particular, may appeal because it calls for exact measurements. Many people say baking is a science, and Virgos can appreciate that. Measuring flour, sugar, and other ingredients down to the gram can feel reassuring. If they want a certain texture or taste, they can tweak the recipe by small amounts. This detail-oriented method helps them see direct outcomes from changes they make. The only caution is that they might get frustrated if something does not come out perfectly. Over time, they learn that small mishaps are normal and often part of the fun.

Enjoyment of Puzzles and Strategy Games

Puzzles and strategy games can keep a Virgo's mind happily occupied. This might include jigsaw puzzles, crossword puzzles, sudoku, or board games that require planning. Virgos like mentally challenging tasks where they can spot patterns. If they pick a puzzle, they might sort the pieces by color and shape first, then methodically build it from the edges inward. The process is slow but calming for them, as they can see the final image taking shape bit by bit.

Strategy video games can also appeal if they do not involve too much chaos. Turn-based games, city-building games, or anything that relies on careful resource management can hook a Virgo's interest. They love analyzing which step is best, figuring out how to optimize resources, and slowly building their success. However, too much screen time could stress a Virgo if they lose track of their daily routines. Striking a balance between digital entertainment and offline tasks keeps things healthy.

Collecting Items or Memorabilia

Collecting objects is another pastime that matches a Virgo's trait of keeping things in an orderly way. They might collect stamps, coins, figurines, or even vintage tools. They enjoy sorting these items by date or category, perhaps labeling each piece with a small tag. They may log them in a notebook or on a spreadsheet, noting where and when each piece was found. This structure gives them a sense of progress. Over time, they build an impressive knowledge about the items, which they might share with fellow collectors.

However, collecting can grow too large if a Virgo is not careful. The desire to have every item in a series can become a bit of an obsession, leading to clutter or overspending. Setting limits—such as focusing on only certain types of items or a particular theme—can keep the hobby manageable. It also helps if they have a designated display or storage system that shows off the collection without crowding living areas.

Volunteering and Service

Virgos often find meaning in helping others. This trait can lead them to volunteer as a hobby. They might help organize events for a local group, tutor students, or do administrative tasks for a charity. Their systematic approach makes them good at behind-the-scenes work like tracking donations or scheduling volunteer shifts. The direct benefit to others is an extra plus, since Virgos like to feel that their time is well spent.

Volunteering also allows Virgo to channel their desire for order into a positive cause. For instance, they might help a shelter keep better records of supplies, or help a library catalog new books. They see quick improvements in how tasks run, which can be very fulfilling. The caution here is the risk of burnout if they take on too many duties. A Virgo who cannot say "no" might end up drained. Keeping a realistic schedule avoids stress and allows them to maintain enthusiasm for the volunteer work they do.

Sports and Physical Activities

Though some Virgos lean toward calm, structured pastimes, others like sports that let them use both mind and body. They might choose activities where strategy is just as important as physical ability, like tennis, golf, or certain martial arts. Virgo's attention to detail means they pay close attention to form—how to swing a racket properly, how to position their feet, and so on. They might practice consistently, keeping a record of improvements in performance or technique.

Still, some Virgos might be self-conscious about group sports if they feel they are not skilled enough. They may prefer solo or small-group activities where they can control the pace and reduce pressure. Hiking, cycling, or swimming can be enjoyable choices that allow them to move at their own speed. Regardless of the sport, structure usually helps—a set routine or training plan suits a Virgo better than random exercise sessions.

Reading and Research

Reading can be a simple yet enriching pastime for many Virgos. Whether they read fiction or non-fiction, they tend to go for titles that feed their interest in learning something new. In fiction, they might prefer stories with careful plotting and well-defined details, while in non-fiction they enjoy biographies or how-to guides that give them insight into the world. Reading in a quiet spot can help them decompress, especially if they have a busy schedule.

Virgos may also enjoy researching a variety of subjects in their spare time, even if it is not for a formal class. They might get curious about a historical event, a scientific process, or a cultural practice, then dig into articles or documentaries to learn more. This self-driven study can become a hobby in itself. Some Virgos keep track of everything they learn in notebooks or digital files, turning their reading into a mini library of knowledge they can reference later.

Music Practice and Appreciation

Playing a musical instrument can be appealing to Virgos who do not mind structured practice. They might try piano, violin, or guitar, focusing on scales and techniques until they can play smoothly. Repetitive drills do not bother them if they see clear progress. The discipline involved in reading music, counting beats, and hitting the right notes aligns with their systematic approach. However, they should remember to let themselves enjoy the music, not just master the technical side.

Virgos who prefer listening might be drawn to music with clear, intricate patterns—such as classical pieces or well-crafted pop songs. They could enjoy noticing subtle layers or changes in rhythm. Some Virgos organize playlists by mood or occasion, making sure each song has a specific place. While this might seem overly detailed to others, it can be relaxing for a Virgo who likes things neatly categorized.

Social Hobbies in a Structured Format

While some Virgos might enjoy solo activities, they can also find pleasure in group hobbies that have a clear structure. For instance, a book club is a good example: it involves reading a chosen book, discussing it in an orderly fashion, and sharing different opinions. The fact that the meeting is usually well-defined—covering themes, characters, and style—can help Virgo feel comfortable. It is social, but not chaotic.

Board game groups or puzzle clubs might also appeal if they focus on strategy rather than purely social chatter. Virgos can engage with others while putting their analytical side to use. They might enjoy explaining rules, ensuring everyone follows them correctly, and then playing with a logical approach. Such gatherings can be fun and still respect Virgo's preference for orderly interaction.

Balancing Relaxation and Productivity

One challenge for Virgos is allowing themselves to just relax without turning every pastime into a project. Their drive to be productive can cause them to feel uneasy if they are not doing something that seems worthwhile. Hobbies, however, are meant to provide enjoyment and downtime. If a Virgo is always measuring results, they might miss the peaceful side of having a hobby. Setting aside moments for purely recreational activities—like simply watching a movie or daydreaming—can help them recharge.

They might benefit from deliberately picking one hobby that has no clear outcome or achievement goal. For example, taking a slow walk just to appreciate the weather, or doodling with no intention of creating a masterpiece. Letting go of the need to be perfect can be healing. Over time, Virgo might discover that this unstructured relaxation actually boosts their creativity and mood, making them more efficient in other areas of life.

Avoiding Overcommitment

With many potential interests, a Virgo can take on too many hobbies, leading to a packed schedule. They might feel they need to master guitar, perfect their bread-baking skills, keep a spotless garden, and read three books a week—all while working full-time. This level of commitment can quickly become stressful. Prioritizing is key. They can pick one or two main hobbies to focus on and let the others be occasional pursuits. By doing this, they maintain the joy of learning without turning free time into another marathon of tasks.

It also helps for Virgo to practice saying "no" to certain requests from others, like managing another friend's organizational project or taking on new volunteer roles if they already have plenty. While it is nice to be helpful, free time can disappear if they say yes too often. Knowing their own limits is an important skill that keeps hobbies fun and refreshing, rather than draining.

Finding Joy in Simple Pleasures

At the end of the day, Virgo's true delight in a pastime often comes from small details. They might relish the scent of bread dough rising, the pattern in a puzzle piece, or the faint color change in a painting technique. These little discoveries make each hobby feel special and keep them engaged for the long term. By noticing the subtle wonders that others might overlook, Virgos find depth in daily life.

In addition, sharing hobbies with friends or loved ones can double the pleasure. A Virgo might teach a younger sibling how to plant seeds properly, or show a coworker how to organize digital photos. These small acts of guidance help Virgo feel useful and also build closer bonds. The other person benefits from their knowledge, and Virgo gets to explain what they do in a structured, easy-to-understand way.

Conclusion on Virgo's Interests and Pastimes

Interests and pastimes give Virgos a chance to explore their desire for order, growth, and meaningful use of time. Whether through meticulous crafts, gardening, logical puzzles, or volunteering, they often pick pursuits that let them see tangible effects. Their methodical style means they can excel at activities that require steps, planning, and careful execution. At the same time, they need to watch out for turning fun into a chore or overloading themselves.

By blending their natural sense of organization with moments of spontaneity, Virgos can make their pastimes both enjoyable and enriching. Allowing room for mistakes, letting themselves unwind without strict goals, and sharing their skills with others can turn any hobby into a fulfilling part of life. Ultimately, the best hobby for a Virgo is one that balances their love of precision with enough freedom to relax. In this balanced space, they discover fun, self-expression, and a healthy escape from daily pressures, all while continuing to learn new things at a comfortable pace.

CHAPTER 16: VIRGOS AND FRIENDSHIP BONDS

Friendships can form a major part of a Virgo's world, though they might not always show their devotion openly. They often bring reliability, practical support, and a calm presence to their friend groups. This chapter explores how Virgos approach making friends, how they maintain those friendships, and the common joys or bumps they might encounter. By looking at both social circles and one-on-one friendships, we see the subtle ways Virgos build strong bonds without a lot of fuss.

Initial Impressions and Cautious Starts

Virgos often take their time when forming new friendships. Instead of jumping into close ties, they observe the other person's actions, listening to how they speak and watching how they treat people. This cautious approach is not meant to be cold; Virgos just want to be sure they are aligning with someone who shares similar values, such as honesty and respect. They might engage in small talk at first, staying polite but somewhat reserved. Over repeated interactions, they grow more comfortable if they sense sincerity.

This slow start can confuse more outgoing individuals, who may wonder why Virgo is not immediately open or chatty. However, once Virgo feels safe, they can surprise people with thoughtful comments or a willingness to help. Friends who recognize this pattern learn that patience is key. Rushing a Virgo to reveal their inner world rarely works. Giving them space to warm up on their own schedule builds a better foundation for the friendship.

Loyalty in Everyday Matters

When a Virgo decides someone is a true friend, they often show loyalty in practical ways. They might keep track of important dates for that friend, such as birthdays or big events, and silently ensure everything runs smoothly. If a friend needs help studying, moving, or organizing a project, Virgo might volunteer without expecting special praise. Their sense of purpose often includes being there for people they care about, and they feel more at ease showing friendship through actions rather than grand statements.

In everyday life, Virgos might be the ones reminding a friend about an upcoming deadline or offering to proofread a vital document before submission. They pay attention to small details, so they notice when someone looks tired, upset, or otherwise "off." A Virgo friend might ask, "Is everything okay? You seem a bit stressed," because they truly notice subtle shifts. This reliable support system can feel comforting, although some friends may need to assure Virgo that they do not have to solve every problem.

Communication in Friendships

Virgos typically communicate with clarity, as discussed in earlier chapters. In friendships, they lean toward honest talks without excessive decoration. They prefer one-on-one or small group settings where they can have more meaningful exchanges. Large, noisy gatherings might tire them out, especially if there is superficial small talk. One or two close friends are often enough for a Virgo, allowing them to form deeper connections rather than broad but shallow acquaintances.

That said, Virgos can be surprisingly warm in quieter moments. A text asking, "How was your day?" or an invitation for a calm get-together can show they are thinking about their friend. They might send a short message with a practical suggestion if they see something that reminds them of their friend's interests. Their communication is often short, polite, and focused on real content, rather than long, emotional messages. Friends who read between the lines realize that these small efforts carry genuine care.

Differences in Social Circles

In a large group of friends, Virgos might stay somewhat on the sidelines, observing and listening. They do not usually aim to be the center of attention. Instead, they might speak up when there is a useful point to make or when the conversation turns to something they know well. This can make them seem quieter, but they are still part of the group, simply choosing their moments carefully.

When dealing with extroverted friends who enjoy being loud or spontaneous, Virgos might need to adapt. They can enjoy these events if they have a clear idea of what to expect. For instance, if they know they are going to a crowded place, they might prepare mentally and set a time to leave if it gets overwhelming. Because they prefer structure, last-minute changes in social plans can irritate them. Understanding that some friends thrive on spontaneity can help them adjust without feeling frustrated.

Handling Conflict with Friends

Disagreements happen in any friendship, and Virgos often try to fix them by calmly discussing the root of the issue. They might recall past details—who said what and when—to clarify misunderstandings. While this method is logical, some friends might find it too precise or feel that Virgo is dragging up old points. Virgos can balance this by acknowledging feelings, not just facts. Saying, "I hear that you're upset, and that matters," before diving into details can help the other person feel understood.

Virgos also strive to avoid repeating the same argument multiple times. They like to learn from past mistakes, so if they see a recurring issue, they may propose steps to avoid it next time. For example, if a friend is often late, Virgo might suggest meeting 15 minutes earlier or sending a reminder text. These solutions can seem controlling if the friend does not see the need. Therefore, discussing solutions gently helps keep the friendship balanced.

Showing Thoughtful Support

One of Virgo's strengths in friendship is their knack for practical help. If a friend is overwhelmed with tasks, Virgo might drop by to assist in a direct way—tidying up, sorting through paperwork, or running errands. They feel content knowing they made a real difference, rather than just offering kind words. However, they should be careful not to assume everyone wants help in this manner. Sometimes, a friend just needs someone to listen and empathize. Checking in first—"Do you want me to help, or do you just need to vent?"—can keep them from overstepping.

Virgo's gift for noticing small signs can also be a source of strong emotional support. If they see a friend withdrawing or getting quiet, they might reach out with a gentle question, "You seem down. Anything you want to talk about?" This can be a relief to someone who needs a nudge to open up. Still, if the friend prefers privacy, Virgo must respect that boundary and not press too hard. Balancing their caring nature with the friend's comfort takes sensitivity, but Virgos are usually quite good at reading subtle cues.

Trust and Confidentiality

Trust is a major element in Virgo's friendships. When someone confides in them, they typically keep that information private. Virgo does not like the drama of gossip or secrets spilled. They value integrity, so they often become the "safe place" for friends to share worries. This sense of confidentiality can draw people to them. Over time, friends see Virgo as someone who will not air their personal issues for attention.

At the same time, Virgos might be hesitant to share their own private matters right away. They tend to hold back, letting others do more of the revealing. Over a long period of trust-building, they might open up about their own struggles, but it usually happens in small portions. Close friends learn that underneath Virgo's calm exterior lies a thoughtful, even vulnerable, person who needs reassurance too.

Friendship Maintenance and Consistency

Virgos are often consistent friends. They may not throw big parties or set up wild hangouts, but they will check in regularly in a quiet way. Whether it is a quick call to see how a friend is doing, a text about a funny anecdote, or an invitation to a coffee break, these small gestures show they care. If a friend has a significant life event—like a job change or moving to a new place—Virgo will offer help if needed.

They also remember details. If a friend mentioned an appointment or a deadline, Virgo might follow up and ask how it went. This consistency can be reassuring, letting friends know they are not forgotten. Some might say Virgo is the friend you do not always see at big gatherings, but the one you can rely on if you really need support. Their preference for smaller meetups can make the friendship feel more intimate, but it also means they might need reminders to join larger social events if they sometimes skip them.

Dealing with Criticism in Friendships

Virgos can be sensitive to criticism, even if they do not show it. If a friend points out a flaw in how Virgo behaves or how they approach a task, Virgo might brood over it, replaying the event in their mind. They might wonder if they let their friend down or if they are somehow inadequate. A good friend can reassure them, explaining that a single disagreement does not ruin the bond. Over time, Virgos learn not to take such remarks too personally, though it can be a gradual process.

On the flip side, Virgos might also come across as critical. Their attention to detail can lead them to point out errors in a friend's plan or to give unasked-for suggestions. Friends might feel judged or think Virgo is always finding something wrong. Learning to phrase feedback gently—starting with what's going well—helps. Also, if the friend is not asking for help, Virgo may need to hold back. Sometimes, letting a friend figure it out on their own fosters respect and independence in the relationship.

Adaptability with Different Personality Types

Though Virgos have their preferences, they can adapt to various personalities if given time. With shy or introverted friends, Virgo might form a comfortable, quiet bond that involves deep conversation or shared, low-key hobbies. With outgoing pals, Virgo might attend events and quietly observe until they find a role—perhaps organizing certain aspects of the gathering or helping with details. As they gain confidence, they might participate more fully, especially if they see a clear purpose in the activity.

One challenge arises when dealing with very disorganized or carefree friends. Virgos may feel uneasy about the lack of structure, while their friend might find Virgo too rigid. If they appreciate each other's strengths—Virgo's systematic approach and the friend's spontaneity—they can create a balanced relationship. For example, the friend might bring excitement to Virgo's life, while Virgo helps the friend manage day-to-day tasks more effectively.

Loyal Support Through Ups and Downs

Once a Virgo is truly close to someone, they can stay loyal through good times and bad. They might be the first to bring soup when a friend is sick or to research options if a friend faces a tough decision. Their consistent presence can feel like a safe harbor. Even if they cannot fix the issue, they stand by, ready to help however they can. This stability means a lot to friends who need calm during storms.

However, Virgos need to make sure they do not neglect their own boundaries. Some friends, noticing Virgo's helpfulness, might over-rely on them. If it turns into an unbalanced dynamic, Virgo can become stressed or even resentful, feeling unappreciated. Learning to say, "I can't help with that right now," is healthy. True friends will understand that Virgo has limits as well.

Quiet Affection and Thoughtful Gestures

Virgos might not be the loudest in expressing affection, but they do so in careful ways. They could remember a friend's preference for a certain type of tea and bring it when they visit. They might recall a friend's favorite author and recommend similar books. These little gestures say, "I pay attention to who you are and what you like." Friends who recognize this pattern see that Virgo's kindness is genuine, even if it is understated.

Over time, these thoughtful actions build a strong sense of trust and closeness. A Virgo friend might not make a big speech about how much they cherish someone, but their steady presence, memory for details, and willingness to lend a hand or ear leave no doubt that they care. In a world filled with fleeting connections, many find Virgo's quiet consistency reassuring.

Challenges with Social Overload

Large or frequent social gatherings can drain a Virgo's energy. If they have a group of extroverted friends who love big parties, Virgo might need to plan some downtime afterward. They do not want to seem antisocial, but they also know too much noise and chaos can be overwhelming. Explaining this need for quiet time can help friends understand. Most will respect that Virgo is fully present when they do join, but needs breaks to recharge.

In friend circles with lots of drama or constant changes, Virgo might feel uneasy. They prefer stability and clear communication. If a group frequently has conflicts or last-minute changes in plans, Virgo could either step into a mediator role (trying to create calm) or quietly pull back. They do best in environments where people treat each other respectfully and keep some form of structure, even if it is a loose one.

Balancing Old and New Friendships

Virgos may have a few very old friends with whom they share a comfortable history. Introducing new friends to this circle might cause them some anxiety. They worry about mixing different personalities or social styles. However, if everyone can accept differences, Virgo might see they have a bigger circle of support than they realize. A well-structured gathering can help ease any tensions, such as planning a relaxed meal where each person can share stories and get to know each other step by step.

On the flip side, if a Virgo moves to a new city or environment, they might find it challenging to open up. Making new friends can feel like starting from scratch, and they might miss the ease of old connections who already know their habits and quirks. In such times, gradually joining local groups or clubs that match their interests—a book club, a gardening group, or a volunteering club—can help them find new companions who appreciate their methodical style. Building trust might be slow, but once formed, it can become just as strong as old friendships.

Deep Conversations and Quiet Support

Virgos often excel at deep conversations once they are comfortable with a friend. They can talk about personal growth, serious issues, or even philosophical topics if they have studied them. Their thorough thinking means they consider different angles and aim to provide reasoned viewpoints. Friends who value meaningful chats can find a reliable discussion partner in Virgo. However, if a friend prefers shallow banter, they might see Virgo as too serious.

Still, Virgo can learn to lighten up by chatting about easy subjects, like shared hobbies, silly day-to-day observations, or pop culture. Balancing serious talk with lighthearted fun keeps the friendship from getting bogged down. Virgo may realize that small laughs and casual topics can bond people just as well as deep insights. They do not have to fix or analyze everything. Sometimes, simply enjoying each other's company is enough.

Respecting Boundaries and Space

Boundaries matter a lot in Virgo's friendships. They want to feel that each person has room to breathe and handle their own concerns. If a friend tries to push Virgo into sharing more than they are ready for, Virgo might pull back. Conversely, if the friend is too distant or secretive, Virgo might worry something is wrong but hesitate to pry. Over time, they learn to gently check in: "Is there anything you'd like to share?" or "I'm here if you need me." This approach respects personal space while showing genuine concern.

Virgos also respect their friend's personal boundaries. If a friend sets a limit—like needing alone time or not wanting certain topics discussed—Virgo usually honors it. They appreciate clarity. As long as the boundary is clearly stated, they can adapt. This mutual respect helps maintain a peaceful dynamic, even if they have different personalities or daily habits.

Friendships Over the Long Term

Because of their consistency and loyalty, many Virgo friendships can last for years. They may not see each other every day or talk non-stop, but the bond remains. Virgos often show up for key moments—a friend's big move, a new job, or a health scare—providing grounded support. This reliability is something friends remember fondly. Virgos might not be showy, but they stand firm when it matters.

Over the long term, a Virgo might be the stable thread that connects different life stages for their friends. They quietly witness changes, celebrate accomplishments in a modest way, and offer help in hard times. Friends learn that Virgo is not the type to disappear when things get tough. Instead, they are likely to check in more often, making sure everything is under control and offering whatever practical assistance they can.

Finding Balance in Friendship Dynamics

One potential pitfall is Virgo taking on a "helper" role too strongly, which can become tiring. If they notice they are always the caretaker, they should try letting friends handle their own struggles sometimes. Likewise, they can learn to lean on friends when they need support, rather than trying to handle every worry alone. A balanced friendship means each person gives and receives.

Also, Virgos should remember that not every friend wants advice. Some just want empathy or a lighthearted conversation to lift their mood. If Virgo sees a friend making what they believe is a mistake, it can be hard for them not to point it out. Yet, sometimes personal experiences are the best teacher, and well-meant warnings might not help. If the friend truly values Virgo's feedback, they will ask for it or show openness to suggestions.

Conclusion on Virgos and Friendship Bonds

Virgos bring a steady and thoughtful energy to their friendships. They might not be flashy or quick to open up, but they show depth in how they care. Through practical support, honest communication, and attention to subtle details, they offer a reliability that some signs lack. Their preference for smaller gatherings or one-on-one chats fosters genuine closeness. It might take time for them to fully trust someone, but once they do, their loyalty can last a lifetime.

By learning to balance their desire to help with respect for personal boundaries, Virgos nurture friendships that are both supportive and free of pressure. They also benefit from letting their friends see their lighter side now and then, sharing jokes or spontaneous moments. Even though a Virgo friend might not shout affection from the rooftops, their consistent presence and caring actions speak volumes. In a world that can sometimes feel superficial, Virgo's calm and dependable nature makes them a much-needed ally—a friend who stands by you, quietly and steadily, through all the ordinary and extraordinary moments of life.

CHAPTER 17: VIRGO AND FAMILY CONNECTIONS

Introduction

Family life can be a central part of anyone's existence, and this is certainly true for Virgo. Known for being practical, attentive to detail, and helpful, Virgos often bring these traits into their roles as children, siblings, parents, or extended family members. In this chapter, we look at how Virgo tends to interact within a family setting. We will explore the ways Virgos handle responsibilities, show affection, and maintain harmony in their households. By understanding these patterns, both Virgos and their loved ones can find better ways to support one another.

Virgo as a Child

Virgo children often display a calm or watchful demeanor from a young age. They might not be the loudest in a group of kids, but they are often quietly paying attention to their surroundings. Parents may notice that a Virgo child likes routines, such as having meals at the same time daily or keeping toys in one particular spot. Consistency makes them feel safe. If their schedule changes suddenly, they might become unsettled. A warm conversation or a clear explanation of why things are different can help them adjust.

They may also show care about doing tasks "correctly." For instance, a Virgo child might arrange crayons in color order or place books in a neat row on a shelf. This preference for structure does not mean they never make a mess; all kids can be messy at times. However, they are more likely to feel a bit uneasy when things are chaotic. Parents who see this trait can help by offering small organizing tasks or giving them a corner of the room to arrange as they like. This sense of order can build the child's confidence.

Virgo children can also be sensitive to feedback. When parents or guardians correct them, they may take it to heart, feeling they failed in some way. A gentle approach works best—one that points out what they did well first, then suggests a small improvement. Because Virgo kids often try to please, they may follow directions closely. This can make them seem extra responsible for their age. Still, it's important to remind them that it's okay to make mistakes and that perfection is not necessary.

In school settings, Virgo children might show strong attention to details, double-checking their assignments before handing them in. They can also be eager to help classmates who are confused, explaining how to solve a math problem or keep notes in order. Sometimes, this helpfulness is well-received. In other cases, they might need to learn that not everyone wants unsolicited advice. Over time, Virgo kids often find that offering help only after asking, "Do you need support?" keeps friendships smoother.

Virgo as a Sibling

When Virgos grow up with brothers or sisters, they often take on a supportive or protective role. They might step in to help a younger sibling with homework, or they may quietly resolve small arguments by suggesting fair solutions. Their calm nature can act as a grounding force in the household. This is particularly true if other siblings have louder or more impulsive personalities.

However, differences can arise if siblings are messy or disorganized. A Virgo might feel irritated when their brother or sister leaves items everywhere. This can turn into mild conflicts if not handled kindly. Virgos in this role might need to learn that each person has a different comfort level with tidiness, and siblings might not see a messy desk as a big problem. Open talks, rather than criticism, can preserve peace. For example, discussing shared spaces and how to keep them reasonably neat often works better than repeated complaints.

Virgo siblings might also be the ones to notice subtle shifts in mood or tone. If a brother or sister seems upset, the Virgo might ask if everything is okay. This level of concern can sometimes catch others off guard, especially if they're used to ignoring small emotional signals. But in many families, it fosters closeness. Over time, siblings often learn they can count on the Virgo for practical advice or a patient ear.

On the flip side, Virgos may hesitate to ask siblings for help, fearing they will burden them. They might quietly handle tasks alone, even when a group effort would be easier. In these cases, siblings can remind the Virgo that it's all right to share workloads and struggles. That gentle nudge can help Virgos realize that family is about mutual support, not just offering help one way.

Virgo as a Parent

When a Virgo becomes a parent, they often strive to be as organized and prepared as possible. From picking the right baby supplies to planning educational activities, they rely on lists, schedules, and detailed research. They might read books on childhood development, compare products, and carefully think about nutrition.

This methodical style can bring stability to the household, giving children a reliable environment.

Still, Virgo parents must remember that raising children is not always orderly. Kids might have sudden mood swings, get sick unexpectedly, or resist a routine that once worked well. Too much rigidity can cause stress for everyone. Striking a balance—having a basic plan but staying open to surprises—helps both the parent and child feel more relaxed. A Virgo parent can learn that small messes or minor rule-breaking are part of growing up, and not every slip has to be addressed in detail.

Virgo parents often place importance on teaching good habits early. They might show kids how to sort laundry, pack school bags neatly, or keep track of homework deadlines. While this can be positive, it's wise to avoid overwhelming kids with too many guidelines. Children need free play too. If a Virgo parent senses their child is feeling micromanaged, easing up and leaving room for creativity will help the child thrive.

Emotionally, Virgo parents can be loving in a quiet manner. They may not always shower their kids with extravagant praise, but they notice and comment on real achievements. For instance, they might say, "I saw how you helped your friend today. That was kind," rather than giving broad statements like, "You're always perfect." This grounded form of encouragement helps children value genuine effort and learn to be responsible. Over time, kids see that their Virgo parent's measured praise means a lot, because it's sincere and thoughtful.

Virgo Interacting with Extended Family

Extended family gatherings, such as large reunions, can be both pleasing and challenging for Virgos. On one hand, they enjoy catching up with relatives and playing a supportive role in planning events—perhaps making lists of who brings what dish or setting a timetable for group activities. On the other hand, the noise and many opinions might wear them out if the event is disorganized or overly chaotic.

In these situations, Virgos may gravitate to smaller, calmer corners. They might chat with one cousin at a time, rather than jumping into a big, hectic group discussion. They also might help quietly in the kitchen, ensuring plates and utensils are in order, so the event flows smoothly. Family members often appreciate Virgo's readiness to step in where needed, though Virgos should be careful not to do all the work alone.

When disagreements arise among relatives—maybe about traditions, finances, or lifestyle choices—Virgos can offer a balanced viewpoint. Their fact-based approach helps them see each side fairly. They might point out the pros and cons or suggest a middle ground that satisfies everyone's key concerns. This talent can reduce tension, although certain relatives may find Virgo's matter-of-fact style too impersonal if they are driven by strong feelings. A gentle tone, plus an acknowledgment of emotions, can make their suggestions more acceptable.

Beyond gatherings, Virgos might keep in contact with extended family through regular calls or messages, especially if they sense someone needs support. They are not always big on casual chatter, but if a cousin or aunt faces a crisis, the Virgo may volunteer to research solutions, look up resources, or provide basic advice. This thoughtful involvement can hold distant relatives together, even when they live far apart.

Conflict Resolution in the Virgo Family

Every family encounters issues at times. In a Virgo-influenced family, conflicts might revolve around tidiness, schedules, or differences in how tasks should be done. For instance, a Virgo parent might become frustrated if a teenager tosses clothes on the floor daily. Or siblings might argue because one is always reorganizing the other's desk. These conflicts typically center on practical matters, though they can still stir strong feelings.

Virgos tend to address disagreements by looking at specifics: "You left your dirty dishes in the sink three times this week," or "Our plan was to leave by 8:00 am, and you weren't ready." This direct focus can be good for clarity. However, it can turn tense if others feel they are being tracked or criticized for small missteps. A helpful strategy is to have a calm family meeting where everyone voices concerns. The Virgo might lead with: "I notice a pattern of undone chores. How can we split tasks more evenly?" This approach invites solutions rather than blame.

When family members show negative emotions, Virgos can feel uneasy, wanting to fix the matter logically. Yet, some problems need space for people to vent frustrations. Learning to listen without jumping in with a quick fix can build empathy. The Virgo can then suggest an action plan once everyone's feelings are acknowledged. Blending emotional validation with practical steps is often the best path to resolution.

It's also important for Virgos to accept that not every conflict has a perfect solution. Sometimes, the best outcome is a compromise or an agreement to let small irritations go. Families are made up of different personalities, and complete harmony is seldom constant. By focusing on workable ideas, respecting each person's perspective, and remembering to be flexible, Virgo's methodical style becomes an asset rather than a source of tension.

Emotional Dynamics in the Virgo Household

Virgos are sometimes seen as reserved, yet they do experience strong feelings. In the family context, they might show love and concern through actions, such as cooking a favorite meal or quietly fixing a household problem. Words like "I love you" might not be repeated often, but their loyalty and attention to daily needs stand as proof of deep care.

Despite this, Virgos can struggle with showing vulnerability. They might hold in worries about finances, a child's well-being, or family plans, not wanting to add stress to others. Over time, this can lead to internal tension or even health problems if they carry too many burdens alone. Family members who notice Virgo's silent load can gently encourage them to talk. A simple question like, "You've been working hard—how are you holding up?" can open the door to sharing.

Children in a Virgo-led family may see their parent(s) focusing on practical tasks, but wonder about deeper affection. Demonstrating small acts of closeness, like giving a warm hug or spending time doing a fun activity, assures kids that their Virgo parent's love is more than just schedules. Similarly, a Virgo child in a family might need reminders that it's safe to express frustration or sadness without fear of letting others down. Finding healthy outlets—like quiet chats or drawing—helps them cope with emotional ups and downs.

Respecting personal space is also a big part of emotional health in a Virgo family. Because Virgos often need a bit of alone time to sort their thoughts, family members can avoid taking it personally if the Virgo occasionally retreats. Likewise, Virgo can watch for signs that other relatives need alone time too. Giving each other room to breathe fosters a healthier atmosphere where everyone can recharge.

Balancing Household Duties

Virgos often become the natural organizers of the family. They might set chore charts, plan budgets, or schedule important tasks like doctor visits. This can keep the household running smoothly. Yet, if they handle all organizational work alone, they risk burnout. It's wise to delegate tasks to other capable family members. For example, if a teen can do laundry, a partner can handle grocery shopping, or a sibling can manage meal prep, the workload becomes more balanced.

At times, Virgos may become frustrated if others do not follow their preferred methods. They might say, "That's not how you fold towels," or "We should store items by size, not color." Some relatives might feel micromanaged. Striking a middle ground is essential. If the goal is simply to keep towels neat, maybe the specific folding style doesn't matter as much. Virgos benefit from realizing that "good enough" can be just fine, especially in a busy family environment where absolute precision is not always possible.

When dividing responsibilities, it helps if everyone has clear tasks that match their strengths. A family member who loves cooking can be in charge of meals, while someone with a knack for finances can track bills. The Virgo's role can be to coordinate these tasks, ensuring nothing gets overlooked. This approach not only prevents one person from doing too much, but also encourages each relative to feel valued for what they bring to the table.

If something is not done or is done poorly, Virgos can still point it out in a kind way. Instead of criticizing, they can say, "Next time, can we rinse the dishes first so they don't dry on the plate?" That phrasing suggests a shared goal of improvement rather than assigning blame. Over time, family members get used to making small fixes without feeling singled out. This fosters teamwork and keeps the overall mood more positive.

Passing Down Values and Traditions

Family traditions can vary, and Virgos often value those that bring order or purpose. They might appreciate routines like a weekly family meal, a consistent bedtime story for kids, or a yearly gathering that happens around the same date. These habits can give everyone a sense of stability and belonging. Virgos usually like preparing for these events well in advance, ensuring that each detail is carefully managed.

While they may not use big flashy decorations or over-the-top celebrations, Virgos do enjoy the thoughtfulness behind certain customs. If there's a tradition of exchanging meaningful notes or reflecting on the year's achievements, a Virgo will likely embrace it. They might even improve it by organizing the notes or creating a simple system that helps everyone participate. Their sense of practicality often helps keep traditions from becoming too expensive or time-consuming.

When passing down values, Virgo parents may emphasize honesty, diligence, and kindness. They want their children to see the impact of small consistent actions, whether that means finishing chores, being truthful about mistakes, or helping neighbors in small ways. These lessons are usually taught through example rather than lectures. A Virgo parent's daily life—tidying up voluntarily, politely addressing others, sticking to tasks—becomes a visible model for younger family members.

In extended families, a Virgo might carry on certain rituals or recipes from one generation to the next. For instance, they might learn an old family cooking method and then refine it a bit for clarity or health reasons. They carefully document each step to preserve it for future relatives. This devotion to detail ensures the family's heritage stays alive, while also adapting to modern needs in a sensible way.

Encouraging Growth in Family Members

Virgos often want to see their loved ones do well, so they might encourage siblings, children, or spouses to learn new skills or adopt beneficial habits. They could suggest healthy meal ideas, educational resources, or ways to save money. This advice is typically given with good intentions. However, if given too frequently or without being requested, it might feel like nagging.

One approach is for Virgo to ask: "Do you want my thoughts?" before sharing suggestions. This respects the other person's independence. If they say yes, the Virgo can go ahead and offer ideas. If not, the Virgo knows to step back. Family members who do accept help often find that Virgo's pointers can be genuinely useful. Because they think things through, Virgos' tips are often practical and clear, making it easier for someone to see improvements.

Another angle is emotional or moral support. A Virgo might notice that a relative is discouraged about a job search or uncertain about a personal decision. Rather than pushing a quick solution, simply listening can go a long way. By asking open-ended questions—like "What worries you the most about this situation?"—Virgos show genuine concern. Then, if asked, they can share methodical ways to handle the challenge. This balanced approach allows for empathy as well as problem-solving.

Over time, a family guided by Virgo's practical input may learn to handle daily life more smoothly. Kids might pick up organizational tricks that serve them well in school. Spouses or siblings might find themselves more mindful of small tasks, avoiding future hassles. In this sense, Virgo's consistent efforts slowly build a supportive environment where each family member feels equipped to manage life's demands.

Shared Leisure and Bonding

Even though Virgos are known for their organized side, they also know the value of rest. Family bonding can include activities like cooking meals together, working on a garden, or playing quiet board games. These calmer, more structured forms of fun can make a Virgo feel at ease. Everyone can follow certain rules and see tangible results, whether it is a finished puzzle or a row of growing vegetables.

Virgos might also plan small family outings, such as visiting a local park or museum. They could research the best times to go (to avoid crowds), pack a well-thought-out snack, and guide everyone through the trip. Some family members love this level of detail, while others might want more spontaneity. Balancing these two approaches can be tricky. One solution is to leave room for unexpected discoveries within a loose plan. That way, the Virgo feels somewhat prepared, and others can still explore in a relaxed way.

When it comes to simple downtime at home, Virgos may appreciate reading quietly alongside a spouse or child, each person immersed in their own book. This might not look like a lively group activity, but it can foster togetherness through shared presence. Occasionally discussing what each person read can spark interesting conversations. The main idea is to find a comfortable pace that suits everyone, without feeling rushed or bored.

Family members who thrive on excitement can still involve the Virgo by allowing them to pick small tasks that help the activity run well. For example, if the family wants to have a larger get-together, the Virgo could organize the guest list, plan seating, or handle timing for the meal. Meanwhile, others handle decorations or music. Splitting roles lets everyone do what they enjoy, and the Virgo's practical nature helps keep the event from becoming chaotic.

Future Outlook for Virgo Families

As families change over time—kids grow older, relatives move, or new members join—Virgos often adjust by updating schedules, household systems, or communication patterns. They may initiate group chats or spreadsheets for planning gatherings. Some family members might find this amusingly formal, but in the end, it often reduces confusion. The key is not to let planning overshadow emotional warmth. Balancing a practical approach with genuine connection keeps the family strong.

Virgo families can benefit from periodic check-ins to see if tasks, routines, or boundaries need updating. Life events like a new baby, a changing job, or shifting health concerns can disrupt established patterns. A short family discussion—maybe once a month—can help everyone stay aligned. The Virgo's role might be to facilitate this meeting, ensuring each person is heard and writing down any decisions. This practice makes the family more resilient, as changes are tackled before they become big problems.

In the long run, the calm strength of a Virgo can serve as an anchor in the family. Their ability to notice small issues early helps keep bigger troubles from emerging. Their willingness to lend a hand, remain loyal, and adapt routines as needed can guide relatives through life's ups and downs. Even though no family is perfect, a Virgo's influence often brings a welcome sense of consistency, fairness, and thoughtful caring.

Meanwhile, Virgos themselves grow by learning that total control is neither possible nor necessary. As children age, for instance, they develop their own ways of doing things. As parents get older, roles might shift. Accepting these changes with grace and trusting that family bonds can remain strong without absolute precision can help Virgo avoid stress. After all, the heart of family life is love, support, and mutual understanding—qualities that can flourish even in a bit of imperfection.

Conclusion

Family connections for Virgo revolve around stability, practical help, and a desire for each person's well-being. From childhood to parenthood and beyond, they use organization and careful observation to nurture relatives and keep daily life running smoothly. While they might sometimes seem strict about details, they do so out of genuine concern for efficiency and comfort. Recognizing the value of emotional warmth and flexible thinking helps Virgos maintain loving relationships with family members who may have different styles.

CHAPTER 18: VIRGO AND SPIRITUAL AWARENESS

Introduction

While some zodiac signs are readily linked with big expressions of faith or deep emotion, Virgo's approach to spirituality tends to be more measured and thoughtful. Being an Earth sign ruled by Mercury, Virgos often blend logic with a subtle sense of wonder. This chapter explores how Virgos may seek meaning, connect with spiritual ideas, or handle personal beliefs. We will also look at how they integrate these insights into daily life. Their path is often grounded and reflective, matching their overall style of taking small but consistent steps toward understanding the bigger picture.

The Earth Element and Spiritual Perspective

Virgo is associated with the Earth element, which often brings a practical viewpoint to matters of faith and spirituality. Rather than diving headfirst into concepts they cannot verify, Virgos typically examine each idea carefully, checking if it aligns with their sense of logic. They may not dismiss intangible experiences outright, but they prefer to see how a spiritual practice relates to daily life. If they find a belief or ritual that provides comfort or practical benefits—like calmness or moral grounding—they are more likely to embrace it.

Many Virgos might say something like, "I need to see how this affects me or others in a real, tangible way." This approach can guide them toward spiritual paths that emphasize service, ethical values, and personal growth. Rather than focusing solely on grand ceremonies, they look for how a tradition's teachings can improve daily routines, relationships, or the community. This down-to-earth perspective can make Virgo's spiritual side more discreet but also firmly rooted in their day-to-day actions.

Mercury's Influence on Reflective Thinking

With Mercury as their ruling planet, Virgos often enjoy learning and thinking things through. This can shape how they explore spiritual or philosophical questions. They might read books on comparative religion, attend lectures, or explore historical contexts behind various practices. Their curiosity prompts them to gather facts and weigh them carefully. They want to know the reasons behind rituals or the logic of certain doctrines.

As a result, Virgos can have a detailed method of spiritual reflection. For instance, if they are exploring a new belief system, they might take notes, identify key teachings, and see how these ideas match their personal ethics. They may talk with individuals who have experience in that tradition, asking specific questions. Rather than simply accepting what is taught, they refine the information until it feels consistent with what they see as truth. This might mean they end up with a personal blend of different teachings, each tested against their own sense of logic.

However, this mental approach can also bring doubt or hesitation. A Virgo might wonder if certain mystical experiences can really be explained by everyday reasoning. They might think, "Is there a deeper reality I cannot measure?" This can lead to a quiet internal debate where part of them wants hard evidence, while another part senses there is more to existence than meets the eye. Finding peace with these contrasting feelings can be an ongoing process.

Potential Paths for Virgo's Spiritual Development

There is no single spiritual road for all Virgos, but certain paths might appeal because they match Virgo's careful, methodical nature. For example, disciplines that involve study and reflection, like certain forms of meditation, can align well. A Virgo might follow a structured practice that guides them step by step, observing the mind without expecting instant enlightenment. They appreciate the fact that consistent effort yields gradual change.

Some Virgos might be drawn to religious traditions that emphasize service or caring for the needy. They find meaning in performing small acts of kindness regularly—helping at a food bank, volunteering in a community group, or simply supporting neighbors with daily tasks. This type of spiritual engagement fits their preference for hands-on help. They see spirituality not just as a personal feeling but as a responsibility to make life better for others.

Others might connect with nature-focused practices. Since Virgo is an Earth sign, spending time in nature can feel grounding. A Virgo might feel close to the spiritual realm while gardening, hiking, or simply watching birds in a quiet setting. Observing the cycles of the seasons can remind them of life's patterns, and they might develop rituals around these changes—such as reflecting on personal goals at the start of spring or cleaning up the environment in autumn. This link to the earth's rhythm provides them with a calm sense of belonging in the bigger order of things.

Still, some Virgos could prefer more traditional faith communities where the teachings are consistent and well-documented. They might like the predictability of weekly gatherings and the clarity of established moral guidelines. Such a setting can give them a feeling of stability, though they may ask thoughtful questions about each doctrine. If the community welcomes inquiries, Virgos usually appreciate the openness to explore complexities rather than glossing over them.

Balancing Skepticism and Openness

One challenge for many Virgos is striking a balance between skepticism and curiosity. Their analytical side may make them cautious about anything that seems too mystical or unproven. If they encounter stories of miracles or supernatural events, they often want to see some form of rational backing. However, if they become overly rigid, they might dismiss genuine experiences that cannot be measured by ordinary means.

On the other hand, some Virgos dive so deeply into research that they risk never fully engaging with a practice. They keep reading more books, attending more discussions, or looking for the "perfect" system. Meanwhile, they avoid actual participation, worried about making a flawed choice. In reality, spirituality often involves a bit of trust—stepping into a method or community and seeing how it resonates over time. Acceptance of uncertainty can help Virgos move beyond endless analysis and discover personal meaning in simpler ways.

Another aspect is being open to small signs or intuitive nudges. Virgos might notice repeated patterns in their life—a certain topic keeps popping up, or they feel drawn to a particular type of meditation. Rather than overthinking, they can explore it gently, testing if it brings inner peace or clarity. This method gives them a bridge between logic and experience, letting them keep one foot on the ground while still exploring deeper possibilities.

Daily Spiritual Practices

Virgos often gravitate to regular habits, so they might prefer daily or weekly routines that keep them connected to their spiritual or philosophical beliefs. This could include brief morning reflections, reading a short passage from a sacred text, or journaling about personal values. By keeping each session structured—like writing three lessons learned from the day—Virgos gain a sense of progress. They see spiritual growth as something that can be tracked, similar to any other skill.

Simple breathing exercises or short meditations can help Virgos quiet their busy minds. By focusing on slow, steady breaths, they can let go of some mental chatter that arises from daily tasks. Over time, they might find that these small moments of stillness bring calm and resilience. While some signs might enjoy long, free-flowing spiritual experiences, Virgo may prefer shorter, more defined periods of quiet. This suits their practicality and helps them stay consistent without feeling overwhelmed.

Acts of service, as mentioned before, can also be integrated into daily routines. A Virgo might commit to doing one kind deed a day, whether that is helping a neighbor carry groceries or sending a thoughtful message to a friend in need. These small but purposeful acts allow them to feel aligned with a higher principle of compassion. Rather than grand gestures, they find meaning in ordinary kindness, repeated consistently.

The Role of Reason in Virgo's Beliefs

For many Virgos, reason and ethics are deeply linked. Their spiritual beliefs often revolve around doing what is right and helpful in the world. They might ask: "How does this teaching improve human relationships?" or "Does this path encourage honesty and humility?" If the answers are satisfying, Virgo sees real value in following those ideas. This does not mean they cannot have profound moments of awe or mystery; it simply means they prefer to keep these experiences grounded in moral or practical outcomes.

Because of this focus on reason, Virgos might be wary of groups or teachings that seem to exploit followers or make unrealistic claims. They tend to back away if they see manipulative tactics or requests that do not feel morally sound. Their inner alarm goes off when something conflicts with basic fairness or honesty. In this sense, their rational mindset protects them from blindly following questionable leaders or doctrines.

At the same time, reason can lead to over-intellectualizing. A Virgo might get stuck in a loop of analyzing spiritual texts without ever feeling a personal connection to the divine or the unknown. They might treat it as an academic subject, missing the emotional or transcendent aspect that faith can bring. Recognizing that not everything can be neatly explained—allowing some openness to wonder—can enrich their spiritual life, complementing their natural caution with a bit of awe.

Emotional and Inner Growth

Spiritual awareness for Virgo also involves inner growth. While they may not show strong emotions openly, they do have a sensitive side. Personal reflection can help them navigate self-criticism and anxiety, two issues that can arise when they place high expectations on themselves. A spiritual framework that emphasizes self-compassion or forgiveness can be particularly helpful, reminding Virgo that it is normal to be imperfect.

Practices like journaling, mindful walks, or simple prayer can help them process emotions in a structured way. For instance, each evening, a Virgo might write down three things they did well that day and one area for gentle improvement. This method is not about harshly judging themselves but acknowledging incremental progress. Over time, it can reduce stress, boosting their sense of well-being.

A spiritual outlook that acknowledges humility also appeals to Virgo's nature. They often do not like grand displays of ego or bragging, so they appreciate teachings that encourage being humble, kind, and service-minded. This resonates with their Earthy quality, which reminds them that everyone is part of a larger system. Recognizing their place in a bigger network—be it nature, humanity, or a divine plan—helps them stay grounded.

Organized Religion vs. Personal Practices

When choosing between organized religion and personal spiritual practices, Virgos may explore both. In a formal setting—such as a church, temple, or mosque—they often want to see consistent teachings, ethical leadership, and a community that genuinely supports each other. They might participate in group study or small committees where they can put their organizational talents to use, such as planning events or managing resources.

On the other hand, some Virgos prefer a personal practice without strict structures. They might craft their own routine from various sources: reading from one tradition, meditating in another style, and engaging in quiet acts of kindness in daily life. This do-it-yourself approach lets them fine-tune each aspect. However, they must be careful not to jump from one thing to another without fully experiencing any single path. Finding a balance—mixing freedom with a bit of discipline—often leads to deeper rewards.

Either way, Virgos usually want clarity. If a religious group states a rule, they want to know the reasoning behind it. If a personal approach suggests a certain practice, they want to see real effects in their life. This clarity can come from trusted mentors, well-written materials, or consistent outcomes over time. Once convinced that a method works, they can become quite devoted, maintaining it with steady discipline.

Handling Doubt or Spiritual Shifts

It's common for individuals to question or adjust their beliefs at various points in life. Virgos might approach such times with a method similar to problem-solving. They could list what no longer seems right about their old perspective and what new perspectives might offer. This logical process helps them avoid panic, but it can also prolong uncertainty if they overanalyze each option. Sometimes, it's helpful for them to let the heart speak as well, trusting feelings rather than logic alone.

During major transitions—like losing a loved one, changing careers, or moving to a new place—Virgos may sense a deeper push to find meaning. They might join a support group at a local community center or read about grief and healing from a spiritual viewpoint. Through these challenges, they can discover unexpected strengths, learning that life's complexities do not always align with neat explanations. This realization can deepen their compassion for others who are also seeking direction.

If they become disillusioned with a certain group or teaching, Virgos may quietly step away, sometimes without making a fuss. They prefer a calm departure over dramatic confrontations. Later, they might reexamine what went wrong, perhaps concluding that the group's actions did not match its stated values. Although this can be disappointing, it can also lead Virgos to refine their own beliefs and boundaries. Each shift, even if painful, can help them grow a more genuine personal practice.

Community and Shared Exploration

Even though Virgos are often independent thinkers, they can benefit from discussing spirituality with a group that respects inquiry. A study circle, a meditation class, or a philosophical discussion group might suit them. In these settings, they can ask pointed questions, compare different viewpoints, and quietly consider all angles. They may not speak up first, but when they do, their comments are often well-thought-out.

Feeling useful in a spiritual community also matters. Whether it is organizing meeting notes, coordinating volunteer tasks, or ensuring everything is in place for a ceremony, Virgos like roles where they see concrete results. They want to feel they are contributing to something larger and not simply attending as a bystander. Communities that appreciate this help often earn a Virgo's long-term commitment.

However, Virgos must remember not to take on all organizational duties themselves. In some groups, the "reliable one" ends up with the brunt of the workload. Setting boundaries, asking for help, and letting others handle tasks in their own ways can prevent burnout. A team approach also fosters friendship and mutual respect.

Ethics and Moral Values

Ethical behavior is a big part of Virgo's spiritual lens. They frequently reflect on how actions line up with moral ideals. Whether they are part of a formal religious tradition or not, Virgos tend to hold strong personal guidelines—like treating others fairly, keeping promises, and being truthful. Their approach to spirituality often includes the aim of "doing the right thing" in real-world situations.

Consequently, they might measure a spiritual or religious teaching by whether it promotes honesty, compassion, and responsibility. If a doctrine encourages exploitation or hate, Virgos feel a moral clash and likely distance themselves. They want to see words and actions match up. If a leader preaches kindness but behaves unjustly, that contradiction can unsettle a Virgo deeply, pushing them to seek a different path or question the teaching.

This moral compass can also push Virgos toward reflection on topics like sustainability, humane treatment of animals, or fairness in social structures. Their Earthy roots remind them of the importance of caring for the planet. If their beliefs guide them to reduce waste, recycle, or help local communities, they see these as tangible expressions of faith in action. Spiritual awareness, for them, is not just about personal peace but about contributing positively to the wider world.

Handling Criticism and Self-Judgment

Virgos often have a streak of self-criticism, analyzing their own shortcomings more harshly than others might. In spiritual contexts, this can manifest as feeling they are not "devout enough" or have not reached the same depth of insight as others. They might compare themselves to people who claim big mystical experiences or unwavering faith. This comparison can lead to doubt or a sense of inadequacy.

A helpful counterbalance is the idea that each person's path is unique, and immediate revelations are not always the point. Small, steady steps—like reading a paragraph of a spiritual text, engaging in five minutes of calm reflection, or kindly helping a friend—can be enough to grow spiritually over time. By focusing on these daily acts, Virgos can release some of the self-judgment that arises when they do not match someone else's experiences.

They may also benefit from mentors or friends who remind them that humility and acceptance are key virtues in most spiritual traditions. Being humble does not mean feeling worthless; it means acknowledging that everyone is learning. If Virgos can let go of the need for perfection, they might find deeper peace in simply trying their best day by day.

Private and Public Expressions of Faith

Virgos may keep their spiritual thoughts relatively private. They might not post about them on social media or discuss them openly at gatherings unless someone asks. This doesn't mean their faith or philosophical viewpoint is weak; it's just that they prefer personal reflection over public display. If they do mention it, they usually stick to simple, clear explanations of what they believe and why.

That said, there can be times when a Virgo is asked to lead a short meditation, give a talk, or organize a spiritual event. Their sense of duty might make them accept the role. Because they prepare thoroughly, they often do a good job, presenting ideas in a logical flow that others can follow. People may admire how they structure concepts, but Virgos themselves might still feel nervous or self-conscious in the spotlight. Overcoming this apprehension can boost their confidence in expressing spiritual ideas publicly.

Friends or relatives might wish Virgo would open up more about their deeper feelings or beliefs. If a Virgo trusts the person and the setting feels safe, they can share some insights. Doing so fosters closer connections, allowing loved ones to see a side of them that might otherwise remain hidden. Over time, these honest exchanges can strengthen bonds and help Virgo feel supported on their spiritual path.

Finding Peace and Inner Calm

Ultimately, many Virgos search for a sense of calm and clarity in their spiritual life. They want to quiet the chatter in their minds, find purpose in their actions, and connect with something greater than themselves—be it universal love, natural order, or a divine presence. By leaning on routines, study, and acts of kindness, they forge a steady path toward this sense of peace.

In everyday life, Virgo might take a moment each morning to reflect on an encouraging phrase, or each evening to note small blessings they witnessed—like a friend's success or a quiet moment in nature. These little rituals do not demand fanfare, but they center their thoughts on gratitude and awareness. Over time, they realize that spiritual growth can be gentle and consistent, matching their Earthy, Mercury-guided nature.

If anxious thoughts rise, Virgos can counter them with grounding techniques: walking barefoot on the grass, focusing on their breath, or sipping a warm tea while observing their surroundings. These simple methods anchor them in the present moment. They learn that calmness often appears in the ordinary details of life, not always in dramatic spiritual events.

Conclusion

For Virgo, spirituality is frequently about weaving logic, ethics, and gentle wonder into a unified whole. They prefer a structured approach that helps them see how faith or philosophy improves daily living. Whether through organized religion, personal reflection, or nature-centered practices, they explore carefully, step by step, seeking consistent truths that match their moral outlook.

Virgos may wrestle with skepticism or fear of being misled, but their openness to steady, practical inquiry allows them to uncover insights in their own thoughtful way. When they find a path that resonates, they often show quiet dedication, upholding routines and performing helpful acts that express their beliefs in tangible form. This humble, grounded stance ensures their spiritual insights blend seamlessly with everyday life, giving them a sense of purpose that speaks to both mind and heart.

By letting themselves embrace small mysteries—things that cannot be fully measured or explained—Virgos expand their perspective beyond strict analysis. They discover that logic and awe can coexist. In turn, their capacity for kindness grows, and they feel more connected to the broader web of existence. For many Virgos, the greatest sign of spiritual growth is found not in big declarations, but in gentle improvements: a calmer spirit, a more caring attitude, and an ongoing wish to serve the common good with thoughtful, well-placed actions.

CHAPTER 19: NOTEWORTHY VIRGO FIGURES

Throughout history and in modern times, certain individuals born under Virgo have left strong marks in different areas of life. While not everyone agrees on astrology, some find it interesting to see if these well-known figures fit Virgo traits, such as diligence, clear thinking, and attention to detail. In this chapter, we will look at a few recognized people whose birthdays fall between late August and late September and discuss how they might display qualities that are often linked to Virgo. We will focus on individuals from various fields, including music, acting, philanthropy, politics, and beyond, to show a broad range of talents and paths.

Before we explore specific figures, it is worth noting that all people are unique. Even if a public figure is a Virgo, that does not mean their actions or personality are shaped only by their Sun sign. Family background, personal decisions, culture, and many other factors influence who they become. Still, for those interested in zodiac traits, it can be entertaining to see if a Virgo's traditional strengths—helpfulness, thoroughness, steady work ethic—show up in the accomplishments or personal styles of well-known people.

Music and Performance

Many Virgo performers in music are known for their drive and methodical practice. One figure often linked to Virgo is the singer Beyoncé, born on September 4. She has been praised for her focused approach to her craft. For many years, she has been said to rehearse extensively before tours or events, paying attention to dance steps, lighting cues, and vocal arrangements. Her performances show an eye for detail that might align with typical Virgo thoroughness.

Observers note that her behind-the-scenes work ethic can be as impressive as her onstage presence. Some accounts say that she will perform sections of a show multiple times to ensure it meets her standards. Additionally, her music videos and stage designs often involve carefully planned visual elements. While she has a strong creative flair, she also tends to manage or co-manage projects, giving input on costumes, makeup, and overall direction. This blend of art and precise oversight can resonate with Virgo's knack for mixing creativity with systematic thought.

Another musical legend tied to Virgo is Michael Jackson, born on August 29. While he is seen in many ways, some fans point out that his perfectionist streak and strong desire to improve his craft suggest possible Virgo traits. He was known for practicing dance moves until they were crisp and well-coordinated, leading to polished stage acts. He also oversaw recording sessions in great detail, giving feedback on every layer of a song. Though his life included many complexities, from a purely performance standpoint, the notion of repeated practice and exacting standards might fit certain Virgo characteristics.

Acting and Film

Some Virgo actors stand out for their thorough preparation and the calm care they bring to their roles. Keanu Reeves, born on September 2, is sometimes described as polite, thoughtful, and dedicated on film sets. While he remains fairly private, remarks from his colleagues often mention that he arrives prepared, stays modest, and invests effort into learning the required skills for a role. For instance, he is well-known for doing extensive training for action scenes, such as in the "John Wick" series, where he spent many hours mastering martial arts techniques and weapons handling.

Reeves's approach could be viewed as reflecting a Virgo-like methodical style: not flaunting success openly but letting his work speak. Interviews suggest he pays attention to daily tasks without much showiness. He also is known for quiet acts of kindness, like giving gifts to crew members or taking pay cuts so production teams can hire top talent. While we cannot say for sure that his zodiac sign shapes these behaviors, fans enjoy seeing the idea of a gentle, service-oriented approach that aligns with certain Virgo themes.

Actress and activist Zendaya, born on September 1, has also been tied to Virgo qualities. She has earned praise for her calm and prepared presence in the entertainment industry. Though young, she has taken on serious roles, spoken about self-image, and shown that she can balance multiple responsibilities—acting, singing, producing, and more. Her attention to detail can be seen in how she manages her personal style or takes part in shaping the projects she works on. Fans often note her thoughtful interviews, in which she chooses words with care, again hinting at the organized and well-reasoned traits that can be linked to Virgo.

Humanitarian Work and Service

Some Virgos have made their mark in service roles, reflecting the sign's traditional link to helping others. One strong example is Mother Teresa, born on August 26. She became known worldwide for her work with the poor and sick in India. Regardless of one's faith, many see her as a symbol of quiet kindness and humility. Her approach to caring for those in need—focusing on direct service and daily tasks—suits the notion of Virgo's practicality in tending to real-world problems.

Mother Teresa's daily routine often involved tasks such as cleaning wounds, distributing food, and comforting the ill. She was not known for seeking attention for herself, and her life remains an example of steady, humble service. Even in her public addresses, she spoke simply, encouraging people to do small acts of kindness each day. While there is debate over the larger aspects of her work and the organization she led, the fact remains that she demonstrated certain qualities of diligence and an interest in hands-on help, which many associate with Virgo's emphasis on real, tangible aid.

Another figure who might show a service-minded side is Prince Harry, born on September 15. Though his life is far different from Mother Teresa's, some note that he has become involved in various charitable efforts, including supporting wounded military veterans and spotlighting mental health. Over time, his public image has shifted from being seen as a carefree royal to someone who invests considerable time in philanthropic initiatives. Of course, there are many factors in such a life, but the idea that he has used a portion of his position to foster helpful causes aligns with the concept of Virgo's drive to do something meaningful and supportive.

Politics and Leadership

Some Virgos in political or leadership roles are described as methodical thinkers. President Lyndon B. Johnson of the United States, born on August 27, is an example, though he is a complicated figure. He was known for pushing forward legislation like civil rights reforms and anti-poverty measures, though critics highlight his involvement in the Vietnam War. Still, from a policy standpoint, he approached matters with some emphasis on details—particularly in domestic programs such as "Great Society" plans. Whether or not he reflected other Virgo traits, such as modesty or service, is open to debate, given the complexities of politics.

Another political figure is Bernie Sanders, born on September 8. He has built a career on detailed policy proposals that focus on economic fairness, healthcare, and education. Followers often appreciate his willingness to outline specifics of how changes might be made, such as explaining funding or legislative steps. While any politician might or might not exhibit Virgo traits, the public perception of him includes determination, thorough policy ideas, and a sense of commitment to real structural reform—some might connect that with Virgo's drive for better systems in the world.

Literature and Writing

The realm of literature also includes Virgos who have left significant legacies. For example, Leo Tolstoy, born on September 9 (old-style date; the new style is in early September but typically aligns with Virgo), was a Russian author recognized for his deep explorations of morality, social structures, and spiritual concerns in novels like "War and Peace" and "Anna Karenina." Tolstoy's writing showed a keen observation of everyday life, with detailed descriptions of characters' thoughts and surroundings. While it is an oversimplification to tie his entire writing style to astrology, the combination of moral depth and precise attention to how individuals behave might fit some definitions of Virgo's approach.

In English literature, Mary Shelley, born on August 30, is celebrated for writing "Frankenstein" at a very young age. Her novel introduced ideas about human creativity, ethics, and responsibility. She was also a careful editor of her husband Percy Bysshe Shelley's works. Some might argue that her method of writing—a thoughtful and systematic approach to themes of science and morality—can show a certain Virgo-like mindset. Of course, she lived in an era with different norms, so linking her personality strictly to zodiac ideas is not exact. Still, admirers of astrology enjoy spotting patterns in her life: a reflective nature and a willingness to examine moral questions in meticulous detail.

Scientific and Analytical Minds

While Virgos are sometimes described as leaning toward the humanities and social service, there are also scientific and analytical thinkers with Virgo birthdays. For example, physicist Johann Gottfried Galle, born on September 9, discovered the planet Neptune. Though not as famous as some other scientists, his attention to precise calculations reflects a methodical approach. In more modern contexts, one might look at various researchers or mathematicians born under Virgo and see if they share traits like systematic thinking and strong attention to detail.

In technology, Larry Ellison, born on August 17, is sometimes mistakenly placed as a Virgo, but in fact, that date falls under Leo. This shows how easy it is to mislabel people if one only uses approximate birth dates. Nevertheless, there may be other true Virgo innovators in tech or science, though they might not have as strong a public presence. Whether they are recognized or not, we can guess they bring the typical Virgo discipline to data analysis, problem-solving, and invention.

Sports and Precision

Some sports figures born under Virgo might showcase steady training and discipline. For example, tennis champion Serena Williams was born on September 26, which actually puts her under Libra, so she is not a Virgo. This reminds us how one must check exact dates. That said, many sports professionals with birthdays falling between late August and late September might exhibit a careful approach to practice, focusing on incremental improvement.

An example is golfer Rory McIlroy, born on May 4, which again is not Virgo. This underscores the importance of verifying birthdays carefully. Alternatively, baseball star Derek Jeter, born on June 26, is also not a Virgo. These mistakes are easy to make if we only recall rough times of the year. The main idea is that for any pro athlete who is indeed a Virgo, fans might see consistent training and a dedication to technique. The athlete may concentrate on daily routines, correct form, and strategic thinking to maintain peak performance. For thoroughness, one must check a valid birthday list to confirm an athlete's sign.

Business and Entrepreneurship

Some Virgo entrepreneurs might run businesses with a strong emphasis on product quality and organization. They might also manage operations in a hands-on way. For instance, Jack Ma of Alibaba was born on September 10. He is described as a visionary, but his company also uses careful data analysis and systematic processes. While many companies rely on logic and data, some see parallels between Jack Ma's approach and Virgo's detail-oriented style: listening to the market, refining business models, and pushing for improvements step by step.

However, real success in business rarely depends on one trait alone, and it is wise to note that factors like market timing and team efforts matter a great deal. Still, when hearing interviews with certain Virgo founders or CEOs, one might pick up on a clear communication style or a drive to make processes as efficient as possible. They usually talk about structured planning and the importance of refining small details that others might ignore. This approach can echo what is typically associated with Virgo's practicality.

Balancing Public Image and Personal Traits

It is helpful to remember that public figures often build a brand or persona that does not always reflect who they are behind closed doors. A Virgo performer might show one face to the media—perhaps calm and detail-focused—while dealing with entirely different personal struggles in private. The same goes for politicians or business leaders. Still, in interviews or official statements, we might see flashes of Virgo-like preference for clarity, thorough planning, or a desire to serve.

When fans or observers try to link celebrity behaviors to astrological signs, they must do so with caution. Not every trait commonly linked to Virgo will appear in every Virgo figure. Further, many individuals have other influences in their natal charts if one follows astrology fully. For example, one might have a Moon sign or rising sign that shapes behavior as well. But if we accept the simple premise of the Sun sign in broad strokes, we can spot mild links in how these public individuals handle their work or present themselves.

Lessons from Virgo Achievers

Regardless of one's stance on astrology, there is often a lesson in observing the paths of recognized Virgo personalities. Many of these individuals show that consistent effort, a practical approach to problem-solving, and dedication to small steps can yield major outcomes over time. Whether it is a musician crafting an album, an actor preparing for a role, or a philanthropist building a humanitarian organization, the presence of a methodical plan can help convert ideas into tangible projects.

Some Virgos also demonstrate the balancing act between caring for one's craft and caring for others. Figures like Mother Teresa or philanthropic celebrities might highlight the sign's concern for day-to-day service. Others, like authors or scientists, point out that fine-tuned observation can uncover insights that benefit the wider community. Even business leaders might remind us that focusing on quality and a well-organized system can make products and services more useful to society.

At the same time, these stories hint at the pitfalls of overwork or perfectionism. Public figures such as Michael Jackson illustrate that an extreme search for flawlessness can bring pressure and personal strain. The tension between excellence and self-care is something that real individuals—not just famous ones—grapple with. For Virgos who identify strongly with the sign, it can be a reminder to find a healthy limit: to pursue mastery but also allow moments of rest and acceptance of minor flaws.

Reflecting on Virgo Figures

As we see, the Virgo Sun sign has been tied to many public personalities across music, film, politics, writing, business, and humanitarian efforts. Of course, each person's path is shaped by far more than a birth date. Yet it can be worthwhile to observe how certain traits—such as discipline, attention to detail, and a service-oriented mindset—keep showing up in these stories. Such similarities may or may not be attributed to astrology, depending on one's perspective, but they do speak to the lasting value of steady work and thoughtful living.

For someone who identifies with Virgo or is curious about it, these famous examples can offer motivation. Seeing that stars or leaders with a possible Virgo style have achieved big things might spark new ideas about how to handle personal goals or creative pursuits. A musician might practice with more dedication, recalling how other Virgo performers drilled their routines. A budding entrepreneur might structure finances and operations carefully, taking cues from known Virgo business founders. While we must all follow our own path, glimpses into others' approaches can be valuable guides.

Final Thoughts on Noteworthy Virgo Figures

Summarizing the impact of these Virgo figures: they span a broad range of talents and callings. Each shows, in a distinct way, that slow, regular effort can have a major influence on arts, politics, social betterment, or scholarship. They also demonstrate that a keen eye for specifics—whether in performance, writing, policy, or organization—can set the stage for real achievements. At the same time, their stories remind us that no approach is free from challenges. Some have faced controversies or personal struggles, underscoring that hard work and thoroughness do not shield a person from life's difficulties.

Nonetheless, from Beyoncé's meticulous show planning to Mother Teresa's daily acts of kindness, or from Keanu Reeves's calm approach to filming to a politician's drive for structured change, these examples highlight the versatility that is often linked to Virgo. They balance efficiency with creativity, logic with service, or ambition with moral reflection—each in their own unique way. Studying these individuals can inspire everyday people to find their own balance, applying Virgo's steady skill set to whatever calling they pursue. After all, the heart of Virgo qualities—practical care for oneself and others—can be applied in any field.

As we finish this look at notable Virgos, remember that the sign alone does not define them. Yet for many observers, the Virgo focus on improvement, precise skill, and sincere helpfulness is plain to see. Whether you believe in astrology or just appreciate good role models, these figures stand as reminders of how thorough planning, mindful daily habits, and an eye for small but important details can build a lasting legacy. They offer clear testimony that even in a fast-changing world, the careful approach of Virgo can still bring resilience, steady growth, and meaningful impact.

CHAPTER 20: THE FUTURE PATH FOR VIRGO

Introduction

Having examined many sides of Virgo—from personality traits and personal relationships to career, health, and spiritual awareness—we now turn to what might lie ahead for those who relate strongly to this sign. In this final chapter, we will look at possible directions, fresh ideas, and areas of life that Virgos might explore. Rather than revisiting earlier detailed advice, we will consider broad themes that can help a Virgo (or anyone seeking to apply Virgo-like qualities) adapt to modern realities and remain balanced over time.

Adapting to a Changing World

Life continues to shift rapidly, thanks to technology, evolving social norms, and global changes. For Virgos, who enjoy structure and clear methods, this can pose new puzzles. They might need to handle unpredictable events more often, rethinking carefully planned routines. These shifting conditions can challenge them to maintain their sense of order without becoming overwhelmed by stress. In the future, Virgos might adapt by improving their flexibility, learning to let go of minor details when necessary, and focusing on core values rather than fixed routines.

That does not mean Virgo must abandon their love of organization. Instead, they can refine existing habits to handle changes with minimal disruption. For example, they might use digital tools that allow for quick schedule updates, or keep more flexible to-do lists that highlight priority tasks first. If unexpected events arise, they can switch or reorder tasks without feeling that everything is ruined. This skill of balancing structure with adaptability can give Virgos an advantage in a world that often demands fast reactions.

Technology and Productivity

Virgos tend to enjoy tasks where they can see tangible progress. The future likely brings more digital platforms to handle work, connect with people, and manage personal projects. While technology can sometimes feel chaotic, Virgos might excel by learning advanced features of productivity apps or using new software that organizes data or tasks. They can carefully filter which tools truly help rather than adopting every trend.

However, it is easy for Virgos to become stuck perfecting technology setups—customizing categories, labels, or color codes. This can lead to a cycle of constant tweaking without real progress on bigger goals. To avoid that, they can set a strict limit on how much time they spend refining their digital systems. Once the system is good enough, they can focus on actual tasks. Over the long term, a balanced approach to tech can help Virgo remain on top of responsibilities, reduce wasted time, and still keep a personal sense of calm.

Evolving Career Landscapes

Workplaces are changing at a fast pace, with more remote options, freelance roles, and team-based environments. Many Virgos thrive in settings where they can bring order to complex projects. They might excel at data analytics, project management, editing, or user experience design. As more companies rely on detail-focused professionals to keep operations running smoothly, Virgos can find positions that let them apply their methodical thinking.

Yet, future careers may also demand creativity and communication skills. Virgos who strengthen their ability to brainstorm and share ideas openly can stand out. For instance, a Virgo might join a cross-functional team that needs someone to coordinate tasks, ensure quality, and also help shape new concepts. This can blend the best of Virgo's thorough approach with the creative spark that often emerges when different minds work together.

Self-employment is another potential path. Many Virgos like the idea of controlling their environment and work schedules. By setting up a small business—whether it is consulting, online retail, or specialized services—they can apply their talent for organization and quality control. The challenge lies in marketing and networking, which may not always come naturally to a private or reserved Virgo. Strengthening these areas, either by partnering with a more outgoing individual or by carefully learning promotion skills, could ensure steady growth in a business run by a Virgo.

Lifelong Learning and Skills

Virgos naturally like to learn. Going forward, this can remain a key advantage in a world that evolves quickly. They can stay updated on new technology, emerging scientific findings, or social trends. This might mean taking short courses online, reading specialized articles, or attending seminars. Because they pay attention to details, they can identify valuable insights that others might overlook, turning learning into a practical asset.

However, with so much information available, a Virgo might find it overwhelming to sift through countless resources. Building a system for sorting and evaluating data can help. For instance, they might rely on trusted platforms, peer reviews, or subject experts to filter out low-quality content. By focusing on depth rather than endless browsing, they can turn knowledge into real improvements for their professional or personal life. This approach also guards against the trap of aimless information gathering that never turns into action.

Emotional Health and Balancing Perfectionism

As we look to the future, emotional well-being remains crucial for Virgos, who can sometimes be their own harshest critics. The next phase might include strategies for reducing pressure and finding acceptance in the midst of imperfections. One approach is to build short rest periods into each day, whether through quiet mindfulness, gentle physical movement, or time spent with pets, friends, or family. These small breaks can ease tension and help Virgos remain steady when facing tough deadlines or unexpected setbacks.

Additionally, professional help—like counseling or coaching—may become more common and more accepted in modern life. Virgos can benefit from a safe space to share concerns, especially if they struggle with high standards or anxiety. An unbiased perspective might help them see that not every error is a major failing and that progress often comes in small increments. By learning to view mistakes as lessons rather than disasters, they can keep self-criticism in check and hold on to a healthy self-image.

Another long-term skill is learning to delegate. In a dynamic world, no one can handle everything alone. Letting teammates, family members, or friends take over certain tasks can free up a Virgo to focus on areas where their strengths shine. At times, Virgos hesitate to trust others' work quality, but stepping back and giving them a chance fosters better relationships and prevents burnout.

New Types of Relationships and Communication

Relationships also shift with societal changes. People may maintain friendships or family ties across distances, relying on video calls and group messaging. Virgos, who value well-structured communication, can make the best of these tools by setting up consistent times to catch up with loved ones. However, they might find group chats messy or chaotic if many people post at once. Learning to handle that flood of information calmly—perhaps by scanning key points or muting less vital threads—can preserve a sense of order.

Meanwhile, new norms around dating and friendships might allow Virgos to meet people with shared interests more easily, including through online platforms. Still, these methods can also bring confusion, as not everyone communicates clearly. Virgo might rely on direct, polite questions to understand someone's intentions. This approach can filter out unreliable connections and help them find friends or partners who respect honesty and detail-focused planning. It might feel awkward at first, but clarity can reduce wasted emotional energy.

Family and Community Roles

Virgos often shine in local groups or family units because they know how to manage resources and tasks. As future communities face matters like sustainability, healthcare access, or education, Virgo's practical viewpoint could prove vital. They might help plan resource distribution or run small community projects. This is an area where their sense of service can align with wider social needs, letting them see real, meaningful outcomes.

In families, new structures might arise: single-parent households, multi-generational homes, or co-living arrangements among friends. Virgos can adjust by focusing on fair rules and supportive routines. For instance, in a household of multiple adults, they might help create a shared budget or a schedule that keeps daily life organized. Their method can keep stress levels down, as everyone knows who is responsible for which chores or bills. This fosters a smoother environment where each person's voice is heard.

Whether in local groups or extended families, Virgos might also develop their diplomatic side. If conflicts come up around differing lifestyles or beliefs, they can step in with reasoned communication. Their typical knack for fairness can help them mediate, proposing balanced solutions. This skill could become even more important in diverse future communities, where bridging differences and maintaining harmony is an ongoing task.

Personal Values and Spiritual Directions

Shifting times often lead people to reassess their core values. Virgos might find that concerns about ethics, honesty, and tangible help for others gain even more importance. They could become involved in charitable or service projects that address real needs—like tutoring children, teaching skills to unemployed adults, or helping set up local waste reduction schemes. By doing so, they merge Virgo's care for detail with moral conviction.

On a more personal level, some Virgos might deepen or refine spiritual practices. Since the modern era can feel hectic, having a solid moral or meditative routine might give them stability. This routine could take the form of simple daily reflection or belonging to a supportive spiritual community. As new philosophies emerge, a Virgo might read or test them carefully, keeping what is helpful and discarding what feels impractical or misleading. This open yet thoughtful stance helps them remain true to their principles while staying flexible.

Environment and Earthly Care

Given Virgo's Earth link, the environment is a big theme that could grow more urgent. Pollution, climate matters, and sustainable living might become top priorities in the years ahead. Virgos, who are grounded and often drawn to nature, can play a part by supporting eco-friendly habits in daily life. This might involve reducing waste, choosing lower-impact diets, or supporting conservation efforts. They might also share tips with friends—explaining how to recycle properly, pick energy-efficient solutions, or plan water usage wisely.

Because they can be detail-oriented, Virgos might excel at leading local eco-initiatives. Whether it is organizing a community cleanup, setting up composting programs, or working with local officials to improve recycling, they can manage the specifics that make such projects succeed. They could also help track results over time, showing how small daily changes can add up to a cleaner environment. This blend of practicality and environmental concern might become a fulfilling part of a Virgo's future path, aligning personal values with tangible progress.

Creativity and New Hobbies

In the future, many people might face shifting job markets and find they have to explore new hobbies or side projects. For a Virgo, discovering creative outlets can bring a healthy balance to an otherwise systematic life. They might try digital art, music production, or even new forms of writing. Because Virgos like to see steady improvement, they can approach these hobbies with a spirit of regular practice. Over time, they can hone skills that bring personal satisfaction or might even lead to extra income.

Additionally, a Virgo might revisit previously set-aside hobbies in new ways. If someone liked painting in their youth but later got too busy, they might pick it back up later with a more structured approach, setting aside a short window each week to experiment with techniques. This can keep them from feeling stagnant. It also reminds them that personal growth is not limited to career or relationships; creativity is a valuable way to expand their perspectives.

Financial Security and Adaptation

Virgos often pay careful attention to money management. In a future with changing economic patterns, they might remain secure by continuing to save, invest thoughtfully, and avoid risky moves. However, some might take advantage of new financial tools—like crowd-funding or digital currencies—if they find logical reasons to believe in them. Of course, they will likely do thorough research before jumping into any big financial decision.

With many uncertain factors at play, having multiple income streams might make sense. A Virgo could keep a stable main job while developing a small side venture, like selling handmade goods, tutoring services, or freelance writing. This strategy can cushion against unexpected changes in one industry. Because they watch details carefully, Virgos can track income, expenses, and possible profit margins better than many. The main caution is not to overextend themselves, as stress could arise from juggling too many responsibilities.

Community Connection and Mentorship

As time goes on, Virgos may find themselves in a mentor role, sharing knowledge with younger individuals or peers. Whether it is teaching a skill, guiding a local group, or training new hires, they can pass on the structured approach that has served them well. They might enjoy watching others improve under careful guidance. This process can also help Virgos reevaluate their own methods, ensuring they stay fresh and do not become outdated.

At a broader level, Virgos might become key players in building stable communities that withstand social or economic shifts. They can lead by demonstrating a balanced mix of kindness and planning. For example, if a neighborhood wants to start a small library or a resource-sharing club, a Virgo can help design the system, lay out clear guidelines, and track inventory. These small but meaningful efforts can help people band together, which is valuable in uncertain times.

Personal Freedom and Self-Expression

Though Virgos are known for discipline, the future might offer them more chances to explore personal freedom. With more remote work or flexible schedules, they could travel while still meeting responsibilities. They might also find new ways to connect with distant friends, study foreign languages, or do volunteer work across borders. This exposure to different cultures or viewpoints can broaden their horizons. However, they should be mindful of not planning every minute—leaving space for unplanned discoveries can be refreshing.

Another area of self-expression might be found in how they share knowledge online. A Virgo might launch a podcast, blog, or YouTube channel, teaching practical skills. They can organize the content in neat lessons or segments, appealing to viewers or listeners who like clarity. This not only allows Virgo to express personal insights but also fosters a network of like-minded people who appreciate well-presented, reliable information.

Health and Personal Vitality

Looking ahead, Virgos might keep refining how they stay healthy. Future health trends could emphasize preventive care, data tracking through wearable devices, or personalized diets based on genetics. A Virgo might enjoy analyzing these data points, adjusting routines to stay in good shape. The potential trap is obsessing over small changes and forgetting to relax. By keeping the big picture in mind—long-term well-being and mental balance—they can harness new health tools without becoming overly fixated on every fluctuation.

In addition, more people may embrace simpler, holistic methods such as herbal remedies or mindfulness practices. Virgos, with their detail-oriented style, may enjoy learning the specifics of each herb's properties or each breathing technique's effect. This can be beneficial as long as they verify sources and avoid unproven claims. Using critical thinking while remaining open-minded is a path that suits a Virgo, letting them find real methods that fit their personal physiology and daily habits.

Deeper Self-Knowledge

The future also holds the possibility for Virgos to explore deeper layers of who they are. Maybe they question certain long-standing habits or decide to break away from tasks that no longer feel rewarding. They might switch fields entirely, trusting that their transferable skills in organization and analytical thought can help them succeed in something fresh. This sense of personal transformation can be both exciting and challenging.

An ongoing theme could be learning to accept that not every plan will lead to the desired outcome. Sometimes, unexpected changes bring more growth than carefully laid strategies. Virgos can practice letting themselves adapt spontaneously. This does not mean giving up structure; it just means allowing flexibility within the framework. Over time, they might become more confident in responding to life's curveballs, combining steady planning with an adaptable mindset.

Social Media and Influence

Social media will likely remain or even intensify in the future. For Virgos, who value authenticity, this can be tricky. Some might decide to keep limited social profiles, sharing only what feels meaningful and true. Others might find ways to use social platforms in a methodical style, posting helpful guides or tips, curated with care. This can build a following that appreciates clarity and real substance, rather than empty showmanship.

However, social media can also feed into comparison and self-criticism. Virgos must be mindful not to measure themselves against perfectly curated images or the apparent achievements of others. Setting boundaries—such as specific times to be online or a limit on daily scrolling—can keep mental health stable. They might also un-follow accounts that trigger stress or negativity. This leaves room for purposeful digital engagement instead of passive consumption that increases doubt or worry.

Generational Shifts and Mentoring the Young

Younger generations may bring fresh perspectives, while older generations can share wisdom. Virgos often bridge these gaps well by translating big ideas into workable plans. In the years to come, they might serve as mentors for younger people who have passion but need guidance on how to implement changes. Virgo's combination of structure and willingness to listen can help new leaders grow responsibly.

Meanwhile, Virgos can learn from the creativity and boldness of youth. By teaming up, they can form partnerships where the younger person sparks new ideas, and the Virgo organizes them into steps. Such intergenerational cooperation might produce solid improvements in social causes, tech startups, educational programs, or local activism. This synergy is something that can define Virgo's role in future communities: bridging energy with method.

Resilience and Long-Term Well-Being

In looking ahead, resilience stands out as a key trait. Virgos already have an advantage here, thanks to a grounded nature that can keep them steady under stress. Building resilience also means handling failure in a healthy way. Whether a Virgo tries a new job that does not work out or invests in something that flops, they can treat the experience as data to learn from rather than a permanent defeat. This approach fosters emotional endurance.

As they move forward, Virgos might also refine the art of self-acceptance. When they see that they cannot fix every problem or meet every standard, they can still aim for stable improvements. That mindset means letting small errors pass without over-analysis and focusing on solutions that matter most. It can be a relief to realize that no path is fully perfect. Imperfections can spark creativity and problem-solving, areas where a Virgo's mind can shine.

Conclusion

Summarizing the future for Virgo, we see that the sign's fundamental approach—careful planning, consistent effort, attention to daily details—remains valuable in an ever-changing world. Whether dealing with shifting careers, adopting new technology, deepening relationships, or leading community projects, Virgos can rely on their systematic thinking to keep pace. They simply need to ensure they do not let perfectionism or fear of the unknown hold them back from trying fresh opportunities.

By honing their flexibility, they can handle sudden changes without too much stress. By nurturing emotional wellness, they can avoid burnout and remain steady when challenges arise. By staying open to learning and maintaining moral values, they can keep a clear sense of purpose. The result is a Virgo who remains grounded but not rigid—someone who sees that the world's ups and downs do not have to disrupt their inner sense of direction.

Looking ahead, Virgos may find that true fulfillment rests in blending their practical strengths with empathy for others and a readiness to adapt. Whether that means guiding loved ones through tough transitions, spearheading local eco-friendly initiatives, or contributing their expertise in new digital fields, the principle remains the same: small, steady steps toward worthwhile goals can lead to deep satisfaction and real benefits for everyone involved.

In the end, the Virgo of the future might be the quiet pillar in many circles—reliable, thoughtful, and always willing to refine processes to make life smoother. They do not need loud displays of success; their impact speaks through improved systems, well-cared-for communities, and personal harmony. While no sign or approach is without challenges, Virgo's steady approach stands as a timeless asset. They might adapt their methods, but at heart, they will always carry the calm care and sense of order that define their place in the zodiac.

That concludes our look at the possible path ahead for Virgo. By staying true to a thoughtful and balanced style, while welcoming fresh ideas, anyone who relates to Virgo qualities can remain strong and useful in a rapidly shifting era. The future holds countless possibilities—both bright and tough—but by emphasizing steady growth, flexible plans, and genuine care for the world around them, Virgos can keep thriving, doing their part to shape a better tomorrow.

Help Us Share Your Thoughts!

Dear reader,

Thank you for spending your time with this book. We hope it brought you enjoyment and a few new ideas to think about. If there was anything that didn't work for you, or if you have suggestions on how we can improve, please let us know at **kontakt@skriuwer.com**. Your feedback means a lot to us and helps us make our books even better.

If you enjoyed this book, we would be very grateful if you left a review on the site where you purchased it. Your review not only helps other readers find our books, but also encourages us to keep creating more stories and materials that you'll love.

By choosing Skriuwer, you're also supporting **Frisian**—a minority language mainly spoken in the northern Netherlands. Although **Frisian** has a rich history, the number of speakers is shrinking, and it's at risk of dying out. Your purchase helps fund resources to preserve and promote this language, such as educational programs and learning tools. If you'd like to learn more about Frisian or even start learning it yourself, please visit **www.learnfrisian.com**.

Thank you for being part of our community. We look forward to sharing more books with you in the future.

Warm regards,
The Skriuwer Team

www.ingramcontent.com/pod-product-compliance
Lightning Source LLC
LaVergne TN
LVHW012103070526
838202LV00056B/5609